BIRTHDAY 1992

HAPPY Birthday
love Jane
xx

PP.
Sandy

That's Racing

Happy Birthday!
Anna

Lois.

Best wishes
Ann

Happy Birthday!
Best Wishes
Sarah

Best Wishes
Pat.

THAT'S RACING

EDITED BY
PETER O'SULLEVAN
AND
SEAN MAGEE

foreword by
HRH THE PRINCESS ROYAL

Stanley Paul
London Sydney Auckland Johannesburg

Stanley Paul & Co. Ltd

An imprint of Random Century Group
20 Vauxhall Road, London SW1V 2SA

Random Century Australia (Pty) Ltd
20 Alfred Street, Milsons Point, Sydney 2061

Random Century New Zealand Limited
PO Box 40–086, Glenfield, Auckland 10

Century Hutchinson South Africa (Pty) Ltd
PO Box 337, Bergvlei 2012, South Africa

First published 1992

Photoset by Deltatype Ltd, Ellesmere Port, Cheshire
Printed in Great Britain by
Butler and Tanner Ltd, Frome, Somerset

A catalogue record for this book is available from the British Library

ISBN 0 09 177183 8

Contents

Foreign fields

Days at the races

Wheels of fortune

Foreword
HRH THE PRINCESS ROYAL

For over forty years the live export of British horses to abattoirs abroad for slaughter has been effectively prevented by the minimum values regulations, but the single European market from 1992 threatens to jeopardize this safeguard.

The International League for the Protection of Horses is at the forefront of a campaign for the retention of the Minimum Values Regulations which protect our horses from being exported live, and all areas of the equestrian world have rallied to the cause. This book is an important element in racing's support for that endeavour.

The editors invited a distinguished group of journalists and participants to submit hitherto unpublished personal racing reflections. The result is a collection of articles which represent a unique contribution to Turf literature. That all the writers gave their services so readily is eloquent testimony to the sport's commitment to the campaign and the sense of humour required to be able to enjoy any horse-related activities.

I welcome the initiative of the racing world in publishing *That's Racing* in support of the worldwide work of the League, and wish the book every success.

Preface

The idea behind this book is a simple one.

Mindful of the widespread support throughout the racing world for the International League for the Protection of Horses' campaign to prevent horses being exported live from Britain for slaughter on the Continent, we invited a variety of writers and participants to contribute an article describing special racing memories to a book to be sold to benefit the League. (Although the immediate threat of live export was removed while the book was in preparation, the campaign to have the protection of British horses enshrined in EC law continues with sustained urgency.) We stipulated only that the piece should not have been previously published.

The response was so prompt and so positive that it left us in no doubt about the genuine feeling which the interpreters of the racing scene have for the welfare of the sport's most important and most uncomplaining participant – the horse.

But the quality of the contributions added an extra dimension which has raised *That's Racing* above the level of the usual 'charity book' and has made it, we believe, the exceptional volume it is. For never before has such a collection of original material from such an outstanding group of writers on the sport been gathered together, and never before have all the varied moods and emotions of the sport been so memorably expressed between two covers.

All the contributors have given their services completely without charge. In addition, several top racing photographers – Ed Byrne, Gerry Cranham, George Selwyn and Phil Smith – have donated their work, and the picture agencies who have supplied the remainder of the illustrations – Sporting Pictures and the Hulton-Deutsch Collection – have done so without fee. This generosity on behalf of all concerned in *That's Racing* has enabled a substantial sum of money to paid to the ILPH in advance of publication, with the expectation of continuing royalties well into the future. We are deeply grateful to all involved for their generous participation and enthusiasm.

We owe a particular debt of gratitude to Gillian Bromley for the donation of her editorial work on the book, and to the staff of Stanley Paul for the dogged determination they showed in acquiring the book in the face of fierce competition.

Our gratitude is also due to those few would-be contributors who did not make the several deadlines and have had to be left out of this volume. The next time we undertake a similar venture, their contributions should be the first to be delivered!

We think *That's Racing* is an important addition to the large body of writing about the Turf, and we hope you enjoy it.

P.O'S.
S.M.

I. L. P. H.

Founded 1927

The International League for the Protection of Horses

The ILPH was founded in 1927 by Ada Cole, a Norfolk girl who was a friend of Edith Cavell. She was a prisoner with Edith Cavell during the First World War and after the war was so concerned with the plight of the warhorses left on the Continent that she decided to make horse welfare her life's work. Since then the ILPH has been concerned with equine welfare worldwide.

The League has helped to bring about many pieces of legislation in the United Kingdom, including the Exportation of Horses Act 1937, the Diseases of Animals Act 1950, the Slaughter of Animals Act 1954, the Ponies Act 1969 and the Protection Against Cruel Tethering Act 1988.

The League is currently campaigning to prevent the reintroduction of the trade in live equines to the Continent for slaughter at any future date.

The League is based in Norfolk with its headquarters at Snetterton, near Attleborough. It has two Rest and Rehabilitation Centres in Norfolk, another near East Grinstead in Surrey and a fourth on the banks of the River Dee in Aberdeenshire. The League owns about 800 horses in this country, most of whom are out on loan to suitable homes.

The League has thirteen full-time field officers working in the United Kingdom and two in Eire, investigating complaints of cruelty against equines and monitoring sales and transportation. They are also responsible for administering the League's horse loan scheme. These field officers are mostly former mounted police officers with great experience of horses, people and the law.

10

Abroad, the League has officers in Paris with five field officers working from France and a network of supporters throughout the Continent. The Paris office is also responsible for the monitoring of the large shipments of horses that come from South America to Italy about six times each year. The League has further offices or clinics in New Zealand, Morocco, Mexico, Ireland and Israel, and there are plans for an expansion into the USA and the Caribbean.

The aims of the League are:

1 Rescuing and rehabilitating equines found to be at risk.
2 Providing a final 'rest' home for a limited number of equines.
3 Sponsoring or actively supporting all legislation to further equine care.
4 Collaborating with other charities who have a mutual interest in the health and welfare of equines or whose work is closely connected with equines.
5 Providing education on equine care and management so as to reduce cruelty through ignorance.
6 Sponsoring scholarships and projects at veterinary establishments connected with research on equine welfare.

The League is a registered charity run by a Chief Executive and a staff responsible to a voluntary Council which meets four times per year in the Norfolk Headquarters, when all main policy decisions are taken.

Fools' gold

John Karter
A MUG IS BORN

It all began that fateful Tuesday in April. The trap was set and I scurried straight into it like an unsuspecting rabbit. The problem was that I was more than happy to be ensnared.

I blame dear old Grandad, of course. With a sizeable percentage of Irish blood coursing through his veins, it was odds-on that my maternal grandsire would be drawn inexorably to the masochistic pleasures of the Turf.

'Come racing,' he suggested blandly one day in the best traditions of a certain J. McCririck. I was just 15 and had reached that state of burgeoning manhood when I was ready and eager to be corrupted, so it needed absolutely no persuasion to recruit me for this nefarious-sounding venture.

My appetite had already been whetted by Grandad's punting activities which, despite ceaseless warnings to me that it was a mug's game, appeared remarkably lucrative for him. He was not a big gambler by any means, but he had that rarest of qualities, a lucky touch, especially in the big races.

With that beguiling way of the Irish, my grandfather had also stirred my interest in the Sport of Kings by regaling me with fascinating tales of the racetrack in years gone by. There were stories of clandestine rendezvous with bookies' runners on dimly lit street corners, of bloody fights between rival gangs of bookies over racecourse pitches and, perhaps my favourite of all, the occasion when a bookie, having lost heavily when the last-race favourite whizzed in at Windsor, jumped in the nearby River Thames, clutching his bulging satchel, and swam frantically across pursued by hordes of angry punters.

So there I was, bright-eyed and full of boyish expectation at 10.30 on a brisk April morning, boarding the charabanc for Epsom races and preparing to sample for the first time the unique camaraderie that binds together that manic breed of cock-eyed optimists otherwise known as horse players.

On the way to Epsom the atmosphere was one of quiet, good-humoured anticipation. It would be a good and profitable day, of that there seemed no doubt, judging by the confident and know-ledgeable snippets of conversation that could be picked up above the rumble of the traffic. Heads submerged in the *Sporting Life* and the racing pages of the dailies were lifted intermittently to pass on such gems of information as 'Flying Tinker's a stone-cold bloody certainty in the third' and 'Sam Hall hasn't sent Blue Jay Boy all the way down from Middleham just for the air, I can tell you that.'

The thought occurred to me that if it was all so easy why weren't these shrewdies being driven to the races in gleaming Rolls-Royces instead of slumming it with the hoi polloi. There was no place for such cynicism, however, and becoming thoroughly caught up in the general buzz of expectation as the charabanc trundled on towards our destination, I felt my pulse quicken at the thought of the great 'crack' to come.

Eventually the towering monolith of Epsom grandstand loomed into view, dominating the skyline like some massive minaret summoning the faithful to worship. Though impressive at first glance, on closer inspection it turned out to be dirty, cracked and peeling and seemed totally inappropriate for the home of the world's most famous Flat race. Little did I realize just how familiar and significant that crumbling edifice would become in my life.

As we trooped eagerly off the charabanc and mingled with the crowds on our way to the turnstiles, what struck me most was the extraordinary contrasts among the throng of racegoers. All men are equal on the turf and under it, they say, and I was to learn the truth of that statement, in one respect at least. Princes and plumbers, peers and pickpockets – whatever their station in life, they were happy to drop their genes and scrabble around together like greedy pigs in a trough when it came to their common goal, the obsessive quest for winners.

Through the turnstile and into the tunnel that led under the grandstand: I was just a few steps away from destiny. I was keyed up like a two-year-old in the stalls, but nothing could have prepared me for the hypnotic piece of theatre that I would encounter being played out against the panoramic backdrop of the Downs.

That first taste of the racecourse was like opening the door to another world. With its giddy kaleidoscope of colour, noise and spine-tingling excitement, it was a world I instinctively wanted to join. As I stood in the ring and observed the frenetic hive of activity in the eternal struggle between punter and bookie, I was entranced by the realization that fortunes could be won and lost by the width of a flaring nostril as sleek and skittish thoroughbreds, blissfully ignorant of their place in the scheme of things, hurtled nose to nose for the finishing line under the manic urgings of those little men in their technicolour dreamcoats.

Soon the hand of fate was beckoning. With the first race approaching it was time for me to take my first tilt at the enemy. My grandfather always backed two horses in a race – the favourite and his own personal fancy – and seemed to draw with remarkable regularity. If I had stuck to his simple system instead of squandering countless hours on more 'scientific' methods of selection, my bank manager would have retired a far happier man.

Anyway, suffice it to say that from the start I knew better than the voice of experience and set about winkling out my own stone-bonking certainties. The first bet I ever struck was with a bookie whose name escapes me. All I remember about him was that he wore one of those spivvy-looking shiny suits and sported a car dealer's moustache. He was almost a caricature of the traditional image of his profession and had such a supercilious look as he took the two pound notes from my outstretched hand that I was left with the inescapable feeling that he regarded me as just another mug eager to be parted from his cash.

The horse had a Spanish name – Feliz Cumpleanos, I believe. The bookie made a half-hearted attempt at pronouncing it as he shouted the bet out to his clerk and as I mentally called on my elementary schoolboy Spanish to translate it as Happy Birthday suddenly I was the one feeling superior. Not for long, though, as you will doubtless have guessed.

As the race reached its climax and it became increasingly obvious that my Spanish sizzler was about to prove a damp squib, I found myself cursing the pea-brained idiot on top. What on earth was that moron of a jockey doing sitting right out the back, making virtually no attempt to get into the race until it was virtually all over? It was the first of endless occasions when I would blame my losses on incompetent riding, the deviousness of the trainer or appalling bad luck – anything but my own lousy judgement, impulsiveness and greed.

I was 'robbed' three more times in the next three races and soon found myself £8 down, not an inconsiderable sum for a schoolboy on starvation-level pocket money. It was, as I had suspected, just a temporary aberration; the wheel of fortune had begun to spin inexorably in my favour.

My deliberations led me to a nag called Huguenot in the fifth. My reasoning was simple: most of the others had not been out and would be lacking in fitness, while Huguenot had finished second, albeit in a poor event, in his one outing earlier that month. He was trained by John Oxley and ridden by Greville Starkey and was being offered at the remarkably generous odds of 8–1. My £2 temporarily tucked away in the bookie's satchel, I watched ecstatically from the stands as good old Grev, elbows flapping in that familiar albatross-like style of his own, drove Huguenot to the front as the field rounded Tattenham Corner and hung on grimly to the line as his lead was whittled away by a storming late run from the second.

Eight quid up on the day – what a star I felt. For my next trick I would play the lot up on an absolute nailed-on certainty in the last. The good thing in question was called Grand Applause, was trained by Humphrey Cottrill and ridden by none other than the great man himself, Lester Piggott. Even Grandad, who needless to say had done very nicely thank you during the afternoon, concurred that the 9–4 favourite was a lay-down.

It was an afternoon of many firsts for me, among them my first opportunity to marvel at the utter genius of Old Stoneface as he wrought his incomparable magic on Grand Applause. How did he do it, I asked myself as I watched him spellbound. Perched like a hawk above Grand Applause with that famous bottom absurdly high in the air, he didn't actually appear to be *doing* anything as he spirited the horse from last to first in the shadow of the post. The crowd were in raptures as Piggott, impassive as ever, brought Grand Applause back to unsaddle, and so, needless to say, was I. This game was easy, I thought as I sauntered cockily over to the bookie to collect my wad, feeling like Stavros Niarchos and Robert Sangster rolled into one. Overall I was in front by a massive £26 – coincidentally the date of my birthday. As an initiation into the racing game it had indeed been a kind of Feliz Cumpleanos.

On the way home, beer was downed in great quantities and all the talk was of Lester, the punters' saviour. He had pulled them out of the mire yet again. If they had had their way he would have been canonized. Well, yes, I thought, Lester might possibly have had something to do with it; but my success was down to sheer intuitive brilliance. I patted my bulging wallet and congratulated myself on an exceptionally shrewd day's business. I could hardly wait for my next sortie to the track when I would hit those quaking bookies with some real bets.

Oh, naïve innocent that I was; if only I had realized. The old enemy could not possibly have organized it better. To start off with a winning day was the worst thing that could possibly have happened to an unsuspecting sucker like me.

They say there is one born every minute and I had just become one of them. The bug had bitten and bitten deep; there would be no regression and certainly no cure. Racing would provide me with some of the greatest highs I would ever experience and, if I am honest, at least as many desperate lows. Life for me could never be remotely the same again, but to quote the French chanteuse, 'Non, je ne regrette rien.'

John Karter is racing correspondent of the Sunday Times. *Previously he was racing correspondent of the* Independent *and before that served 14 years with* The Times *as racing editor.*

John Tyrrel
THE MINSTREL AND THE MILK GIRL

The seeds of my journey to Epsom to witness the 1947 Derby were sown in the late summer of 1945. For me at least the war was over. Victory in Europe had been celebrated on 8 May, and the continuing Far Eastern conflict seemed remote to a 10-year-old schoolboy who had emerged unscathed from the rigours of Biggin Hill, air raids, doodlebugs and the sheer indignity of sweet rationing.

My father was a keen racing buff who had flown with the Air Force between the wars, mostly in the Middle East; although 1939 found him too old for active service, he stayed in the RAF none the less, and in August 1945 he was on leave awaiting a posting to South-East Asia. It was at this juncture that he decided to introduce me to the pleasures and perils of the Turf. In his 1935 Ford Eight, still in its wartime camouflage, we set off from 'Little Orchard' in suburban Hertfordshire, for Newmarket. The journey, over almost deserted roads, took considerably less time than it does today, and on arrival at the July Course I was swiftly installed at the top of Tatts grandstand, in the far left corner, to afford the best view of the first race.

This was the Tostock (Apprentice) Stakes for two-year-olds. My father departed to have his tilt with the ring, and as the field streamed to post in the hot August sunshine, I was joined by a very fat gentleman carrying binoculars of naval proportions. Needless to say, his ample figure obscured my view for much of the race, won by Pandemonium in the colours of Mr J. E. Ferguson, later carried to victory in the 1946 Derby by Airborne.

The corpulent gent had evidently had a bet on the winner, as he spent the final stages of the race jumping up and down shouting 'Pandemonium for a Pony'. The word 'pony' was a little lost on me

20

as at that time I thought it described a small horse, but the punter was obviously pleased with his plunge on the 4–1 joint favourite, and he positively scampered down the steps of the stand to collect.

Of the budding jockeys in the Tostock Stakes, only John Winter and Jeff Barlow would stir any memories today, but also displaying their talents that afternoon were Gordon Richards, Harry Wragg, Eph Smith, Micky Greening, 'Midge' Richardson, Bobby Jones, Billy Nevett, Doug Smith, Tommy Carey and Willie Stephenson. It was racing with the gods, and from a new found vantage point in the paddock, I saw these celestial beings mount, pull up and unsaddle. It was a close-up of heroes hitherto known to me only through the sports pages, and by the time Tommy Carey had won the Wickambrook Stakes on Despatch Case and Gordon Richards had taken the Rutland Stakes on Naishapur, the Turf had acquired a lifelong devotee.

Pausing only to send me a Christmas coconut from Ceylon (delivered on 25 December, the smooth outer shell smothered in exotic stamps), my father returned from his tour of duty early in 1947, and resigned his commission. Comfortably cushioned by his service gratuity, he decided that this could best be enhanced by a series of investments, not in shares or insurance, but in a three-year-old colt by Owen Tudor named Tudor Minstrel.

Trained by Fred Darling, unbeaten in four races at two and top of the Free Handicap with 9st 7lb, Tudor Minstrel won the Two Thousand Guineas with contemptuous ease at 11–8 on. The gratuity was looking pretty good. Flushed with success, and having secured reasonable ante-post Derby odds before the Guineas, we hired a car and driver to take us to Epsom for the big race – the first I saw and the first to be run at Epsom on a Saturday, a move stipulated by the Labour government in a bid to prevent mid-week absenteeism by the workers.

The June skies were dull, cloudy and intermittently rainswept. Approach roads were impassable over a mile from the course. The car was parked in a cluttered side road, and we scrambled our way to the stands, finally squeezing into the Silver Ring after the first race. Having managed to wriggle to the top of the stand, I gazed out over the Downs. They were black with people. Not a blade of grass could be seen except for the dark green ribbon of the track.

We'd found a racecard seller as we crossed the golf links, and I just had time to note the winner of the first, The Yuvaraj, ridden by Edgar Britt. In 1947, and for many years after, the first two races on Derby Day were over five furlongs, presumably to keep the horseshoe track pristine for the main event. Those were also the days before the advent of course commentators, overnight declarations and photo-finish equipment. Racegoers didn't know the runners until they were hoisted into the creaking number-board about twenty minutes before the race, when they were read over the public address system by the course announcer, who also gave the result, odds and Tote returns.

Seven took the field for the second, the Caterham Stakes. Two outsiders, ridden by Johnny Gilbert and Tommy Bartlam respectively, managed to impede each other at the start, leaving Michael Beary to scoot home on Final Set, trained by Atty Persse. The winner was returned at 9–4 on, and paid a generous 3s 9d on the Tote. The Yuvaraj had also been 9–4 on, and the punters were in a mood to play up their winnings on Tudor Minstrel, now being called in the ring at 7–4 on. I could tell from my father's beaming face as he waved from the mêlée below that he planned to do just that and he had certainly laid a bit on Final Set.

As it turned out, the name was to be prophetic. After what seemed an eternity wedged against the wall of the stand, I heard the Tannoy crackle into life with the brittle BBC tones then much in vogue as the course announcer gave the runners and riders for the 'Debby Stecks'. The field emerged from the paddock, well out of sight to my right, for a perfunctory parade. Tudor Minstrel was number 8, and in the dull conditions the white colours with dark tartan cross-belts worn by Gordon Richards seemed not unlike the white with black hoop sported by George Bridgland on Pearl Diver, whose number 13 could have been 8 as the saddle-cloths flapped in the breeze. However, the potential for confusion lurking in these similarities did not become apparent to the backers who had laid the odds on Tudor Minstrel and neglected Pearl Diver at 40–1 for another ten minutes or so.

The story of the race is easily told. In his autobiography Sir Gordon admitted that he really had no idea of how to ride the horse at Epsom. Trials on Fred Darling's replica left-handed track at Beckhampton had shown that Tudor Minstrel's action was to the right. Leading with the near fore, he was 'all at sea'. The options were either to let him go and risk the leftward bends, or to hold him up and save the colt's brilliant speed for the finish. In the event, it was neither Darling nor Richards who decided. It was Tudor Minstrel himself, who refused to settle. Every time his jockey let him go he darted right, and when held up he fought every inch of the way, finishing an exhausted and undistinguished fourth. He clearly hated the course, and he may well have hated the sprawling, noisy crowd, far as he was from the remote pleasances of Newmarket and the disciplined elegance of Royal Ascot where he had won the Coventry Stakes as a two-year-old.

Meanwhile Pearl Diver, trained by Percy Carter at Chantilly and given his final preparation by Claud Halsey at Newmarket, was always going smoothly under George Bridgland. Placed handily on the outside of the bulldozing Tudor Minstrel as the latter led into the straight, he followed Sayajirao when Edgar Britt took the subsequent St Leger winner up the rails and into the lead with two furlongs to run, and swept past to win easily by four lengths. Migoli, in the colours of the Aga Khan, ran on to be second with Sayajirao third.

Inevitably, in the absence of any commentary, many backers in the packed stands and those craning their necks on the Downs had confused the colours and numbers of the favourite and the unconsidered French outsider, including, as it later transpired, the French radio commentator, who frenziedly told his Gallic audience that Gordon Richards had won his first Derby. The euphoria lasted only until the result was hauled into the frame, creaking and rattling like a gibbet in the summer wind, hanging the hopes of thousands as the Spode-voiced announcer intoned the starting prices. 'Gratuiti in memoria,' I thought, rather pleased with my prep school Latin at the time.

Excitement over, and most the poorer, the punters slowly started on the painful path home. My father joined me through the dwindling crowd to watch Gordon Richards win the next race on the Aga Khan's Usumbura. The champion's less than ecstatic reception was perhaps understandable. Sorrows briefly drowned in the bar beneath the stand, we plodded back to our car and its patient driver, who discreetly asked no questions on the long drive home. Although we could not have known, we had just witnessed a race which was to set the mould of the immediate post-war Classics and what we would now call Pattern races. The former supremacy of the British thoroughbred was to be successfully challenged for many years to come, first by the French, who won nineteen classic races between 1947 and 1959, secondly by the Italians, led by the fabulous Ribot, and thirdly by the North American dynasties exemplified by Northern Dancer.

Tudor Minstrel went on to win the St James's Palace Stakes over Ascot's right-handed mile, but was beaten by Migoli in the Eclipse. A mile proved to be his optimum trip and confined to eight furlongs he may never have tasted defeat.

My father had fortunately paid our driver in advance and we lost no time in stitching on the brave smiles with which to greet my mother in the living room of 'Little Orchard'. She was knitting briskly at the fireside. 'Well, I don't think much of your Tudor Minstrel,' she said, 'but I heard on the wireless this morning that the Queen [now HM Queen Elizabeth the Queen Mother] was off to the Derby wearing her pearls, so I gave Mary the milk girl half a crown each way to put on Pearl Diver.'

I suddenly remembered that school resumed on Monday. It was time for some private revision of Latin verbs.

John Tyrrel joined BBC Television in 1965. He moved to ITV in 1971 and joined World of Sport *as a broadcaster in 1977, becoming a member of the ITV midweek racing team in 1979; he now broadcasts for Channel Four Racing. Author of* Racecourses on the Flat *and* Chasing Around Britain, *he writes on racing matters for* Countryweek *magazine.*

Colin Mackenzie
SUPERFLUOUS

It all began when Nigel Dempster and I decided to try and win the *Daily Express* Triumph Hurdle. We should have known better, of course. Even Martin Pipe will tell you it is harder to win than the Derby. But Nigel and I had our own special reasons for wanting the *Express*'s money. Both of us had started our Fleet Street careers as cub reporters on the William Hickey column in the early Sixties. Nigel had remained with gossip over the years while I had fled the den to become an education reporter and then a foreign correspondent.

The first time I had a runner at the Cheltenham National Hunt Festival was in 1974 when I and my old pal Brian Vine, who was the New York bureau chief of the *Express*, bought a little horse called Overall who won a few novice hurdles and was considered good enough to run in the first division of the Gloucester Hurdle. Sods' Law dictated that I was halfway up the Amazon river on the trail of train robber Ronnie Biggs and so I missed all the fun. Suffice it to say that Overall came in a gallant seventeenth; but our trainer Les Kennard was able to impart the valuable information that Highland Abbe would win the Long Distance Hurdle. This he duly did at the very rewarding odds of 14–1 – which was not much help to Overall's part-owner who was struggling to make himself known to some Guarani Indians at the time.

In 1975 Overall was moved to the Wiltshire stables of one J. A. B. Old, a young man on the threshold of his training career. Known as the duckpond genius, because of Ashmore's most distinguishing feature, Jim was and is great company, with a remarkable ability to mimic senior colleagues such as the late Fred Rimell, Toby Balding and David Gandolfo. He could also train to some purpose and although by now Overall was in the autumn of his career Jim and

25

his jockey Bob Champion seemed to know the time of day. I mention this only because the story now moves on some eight years to 1983, by which time Jim had outgrown Ashmore and was established in grander surroundings at Dundry, just south of Bristol. He couldn't have known it at the time, but the move proved all but fatal to his promising career: in the new yard his horses seemed to be constantly suffering from the virus and/or other ailments, and his scoring rate declined accordingly.

By September of that year I had joined Nigel's band of gossips at the *Daily Mail*. I had resigned from the *Daily Express* some eight years earlier to concentrate on writing books and film scripts, but now with school fees looming large a regular salary seemed to be the order of the day – or so ordained my bank manager. I decided to visit young Old, as he came to be known in the Dempster column, in his new environment at Dundry, complete with all-weather gallop and so forth. Impressive stuff – and Cima had just finished second in the Triumph Hurdle that spring. Any old fool could tell that he was an unlucky loser, too, beaten by the 66–1 fluke winner Shiny Copper. This was the man to bring home the bacon to a couple of former *Express* hacks, for sure.

So who was this gleaming bay gelding being paraded by chance before my eyes – all muscle and lithe movement, the epitome of good breeding and good health?

'This is Superfluous,' announced the trainer with a surge of expectancy. 'I pinched him from Sir Mark Prescott for a knock-down £8,000. He won a nice race at Ayr on the flat this summer and then got a little jarred up. He'll do the job for you perfectly.

'He's owned by Major Jack Rubin – but all his horses are for sale. He'll sell him to you for a small profit, take my word.'

Sure he will. In fact the Major, who sadly died a couple of years later, owned Maori Venture who went on to win the 1987 Grand National. Jim had hoped to keep the horse but he was sold at the disposal of the Major's string and Jim Joel bought him for Andy Turnell. Such is fate in the world of racing.

But back to Superfluous. The Major agreed to take a small profit and quicker than you could say 'done' he was ours. Nigel boldly took a 50 per cent share, while my bank manager insisted that I find two other partners for the remaining half of the horse in order that 16.67 per cent should be my maximum commitment. To this day I feel guilty about it, but I am happy to say that the two people concerned, public relations chief Chris Morgan and Baker Street shop owner Stephen Freud are still speaking to me. Goodness knows why, though.

Late November's Hennessy meeting at Newbury seemed an appropriate place to launch our superhorse. We didn't want to swank too much at somewhere like humble Huntingdon or lowly Leicester. It would be too unkind to the other horses to beat them out of sight – positively cruel, in fact. So Superfluous was aimed at the Freshman's Hurdle on the Friday of this prestigious meeting. No point in messing about – we wanted to announce our presence, though not until after we had availed ourselves of a little of the 66–1 that Mike Dillon of Ladbrokes was fool enough to offer for his March objective.

Like most events in racing the best part of the whole exercise was the anticipation. Strutting our stuff in front of the Newbury grandstand we were an appalling sight, all puffed up with nowhere to go.

April may be the cruellest month according to T. S. Eliot; November can be pretty bleak as well. It took just four minutes and ten seconds for our chimera to collapse, for the dream to be demolished. Superfluous had jumped like a stag. A very slow stag. Graciously, he had allowed his seven rivals the privilege of preceding him to the winning post.

'Showed a lot of promise considering he needed it so badly,' said the trainer – in direct contradiction to his comments fifteen minutes earlier. We've all heard of creative accounting, but this was selective recollection that would shame a gossip columnist! There was only one thing for it: repair to the bar, where the ever-generous Nigel already had a bottle of Bollinger at the ready. If we were going to drown our sorrows they might as well expire in style.

The story now moves on again; some two years, this time, to Kempton on a sunny September day on the Flat. Superfluous never ran in the *Daily Express* Triumph Hurdle, but not for want of trying. We left him in until the last moment in the hope that he would be balloted out and we would recover our entry fees. It was the only time the poor beast was a certainty – and we duly got our money back. The principal reason for this was that in all his outings in the interim he manifestly failed to trouble the judge, indeed, he never once beat another horse home.

Now there are few bigger fools than racehorse owners, especially unsuccessful racehorse owners. They grow unaccountably attached to their four-legged friends and continue to pour vast sums of money into their training long after such indulgence has parted company with prudence. We made all sorts of excuses for Superfluous, whose appearances in the Dempster column as the 'Diary wondernag' were by now strictly rationed. Young Old was still suffering from the virus, or from atomic radiation from Hinckley Down, or from rape seed infection – anything but the obvious, which was that the wretched nag was slower than Thomas the Tank Engine.

Jim decided that despite Superfluous's dexterity over hurdles he was probably more suited to the Flat after all. After a summer at grass the five-year-old had come back fitter and stronger and at home was working like his father Track Spare. A mile-and-a-half handicap at Kempton would restore the horse's confidence and provide his loyal owners with a much-needed taste of success. To eliminate any doubt from the horse's mind about what was expected of him, blinkers were fitted to his handsome head and spurs to the jockey's boots.

By now N. Dempster was no longer strutting his stuff in front of the Members' stand. A chap has a reputation to protect. So he entertained his eight-year-old daughter, Louisa, to a light lunch in the restaurant *behind* the grandstand while yours truly was deputed to witness the greatest comeback since Foinavon. However, Nigel had taken the precaution of ordering a bottle of Krug with which to celebrate the run.

The finest efforts of Stirling-born Mr William Carson failed to stir Superfluous from his accustomed reverie – a discreet half furlong behind the rest of the field. That's where he stayed, finishing about 100 yards behind his nearest rival. As I rose to 'greet' the horse and jockey for a post-mortem I caught sight of Sir Mark Prescott. Remember him? The man from whom we had 'stolen' Superfluous for £8,000.

'Come and say hello to Nigel Dempster, Mark,' I said in my most oleaginous tone. 'He'd love to meet you.'

I could see Mark weighing up the pros and cons of this exercise. He must have been sufficiently worried that the love life of racing's most active bachelor would be exposed if he turned down the request, for he muttered a gruff 'OK'.

As we entered the restaurant young Old was in deep conversation with Nigel, who was pouring a glass of bubbly for him. There was not a lot of laughter.

Mark, who has never been short of a *bon mot*, took in the scene at a glance and after I had introduced him to Nigel gratefully accepted his share of the Krug. Then he turned to Jim and said, 'Christ Almighty – what's he going to buy you when this horse beats one home?'

In seventeen outings for us Superfluous never, ever beat another horse home – which must be some kind of record. But I will remember him long after I have forgotten more successful animals that I have been fortunate enough to part-own. It was just that he was so well named!

Colin Mackenzie is the racing correspondent of the Daily Mail. *He has been in Fleet Street since graduating from Oxford University in 1964 with a degree in PPE and a* penchant *for the Turf which has effectively ruined his chances of becoming a millionaire.*

Geoff Lester
'LISTEN TO THE MAN'

April 16, 1960. It was Easter Saturday, and, more importantly, my dear old Dad's 39th birthday. I had just turned 12, and, having saved up a few weeks' pocket money, I decided to surprise Dad by offering to treat him to a day at the races.

'No thanks son, I hate going alone,' he replied, explaining that Mum could not come, because, with my elder brother Alan doing his grocer's delivery round, there was nobody to keep a watchful eye over such an exuberant youngster as myself.

'I'm coming with you, Dad,' I chirped – my voice had still not broken – 'racing looks good fun on the box and I'm fed up stuffing myself with Easter eggs.'

Mum and Dad had a brief 'Stewards' Enquiry' before declaring the thumbs up, and, bicycles at the ready, the Lester father and son team were soon *en route* to Kempton Park from our Twickenham base, some five miles away. Sandwiches neatly packed in our saddle-bags, we pedalled down the back lanes to avoid the heavy traffic of the Chertsey Road and arrived at the Sunbury course in good time to padlock our 'mounts' for the statutory one shilling charge at one of the houses opposite the track.

Dad was an infrequent racegoer and he normally opted for the Silver Ring rather than Tatts or Members, but my pocket was even thinner than his and would not stretch to 'the silver', so we headed for the Cheap Enclosure, where entrance to the far side of the course was only two bob for adults and free for kids.

Out in the middle of the track was the legendary tipster, Ras Prince Monolulu, plying his trade in his colourful feathered headdress.

'I've gotta horse,' he screamed, and eager punters did not have to think twice before thrusting a pound note his way to find out the name of the day's 'good thing'. Across the track, however, was

30

another tipster, seeking out the mugs, and, while he did not have the colourful charismatic charm of 'The Prince', he was only charging half a crown for a piece of paper which allegedly contained three certainties. My old Dad was a sucker for such a 'bargain'. I tried to tell him that if this middle-aged man, who called himself Curley (he had a mop of curly black hair and bore no resemblance to Barney), really knew of three steering jobs, he would not be so shabbily dressed in a dusty grey suit and moth-eaten trilby.

'Shh, listen to the man,' said Dad, reprimanding me, and Curley, who, by now, had attracted an audience of around a dozen, was pacing up and down, informing us that he was 'on the course at 6.30 that morning, watching some of today's runners having their final workouts'. Too naïve to realize that such claims had to be hogwash, I had to agree with Dad that Curley sounded impressive, so, between us, we risked 2s 6d and sloped off into a quiet corner to open our secret envelope.

True to his word, Curley had scribbled down three names – and, beside them, he had even told us why they would win! First there was Snowy Parker's Falls of Shin in the Rosebery Handicap: 'Sanctum will be short, but Lester Piggott rides ours and they went like a rocket on a spin on the course before breakfast,' he wrote. Secondly, Nice Guy in the Two Thousand Guineas Trial: 'I saw all the horses on the track this morning and this Irish raider, the mount of Tommy Gosling, is far and away the fittest. Don't miss him,' pleaded Curley. And thirdly, Soldanella in the last: 'Piggott rides, and he'll be any price.'

We sat down, and while devouring Mum's corned beef and beetroot sandwiches I thumbed through my *Sporting Life* – I had heard it was the racing Bible and a priest would not go into church without the tools of the trade – and began to evaluate the chances of landing the treble chance. According to Man on the Spot, Falls of Shin (10–1) and Nice Guy (100–8) both had a squeak, though little more than that, but Soldanella was 20–1 – surely that Curley was having us on!

Whenever he went racing my Dad had to have a bet in every contest, so, while Falls of Shin was not running until the third, his first priority was to find the winner of the opener, a seller. Being a confirmed favourite-backer, the thought of missing Badmash when the bookies were going 9–4 and 6–1 bar never entered his mind; we hurried off to put our 4s on the Tote and raced down to the mile-and-a-half start. Terry Stringer broke well on Badmash, who carried the colours of subsequent St Leger winner Sodium, and we hared back towards the winning post just in time to see the 'jolly' sail past in front. And he paid 3–1 on the 'nanny'.

The handful of bookies over the far side were doing a roaring Bank Holiday trade, none more so than a scruffy old man who traded in a ramshackle hut and was assisted by an equally ancient woman with holes in her sandals. Inquisitive racegoers huddled around this octogenarian pair, and the toothless layer cried: 'Don't say you can't get on with Nobby and Florrie. Anything down to a tanner, and each way as well. We'll take it.' Intent on playing up his winnings – the slow queues at the Tote window meant that we only collected minutes before the off of the next race (hooray for new technology) – Dad had watched Sam Armstrong's Palatina be backed from 7–4 to 11–10 on. With Piggott aboard, it was too good to let go unbacked, so he persuaded Nobby to lay him an even 10s and then promptly looked down at me and said: 'Don't tell Mum!' I told him that if he put my 5s on Palatina as the first leg of the Tote Treble I would not utter a word. We both got a pitch by the rails of the straight course and roared ourselves hoarse as the favourite skated up by four lengths.

For a kid let loose on a racecourse for the first time, I could not believe my luck. I had cracked it – I had the bookies by the short and curlies!

Now for Falls of Shin. Dad, wallowing in the fact that the first two favourites had gone in, was becoming a bit of a 'doubting Thomas' and, wobbling as he saw the cash flooding on Breasley and Sanctum, just as Curley had predicted, he decided to follow the money. However, I could not see the point in paying the half crown for Curley's tips if we were not going to give the poor fellow a chance, so, accompanying Dad's 15s–10s on Sanctum, I hit Nobby with 'ten dollars' Falls of Shin on the same ticket.

In a four-way blanket finish of heads and short heads, the then not-so-old Piggott didn't let me down; squeezing through on the fence, he lifted Falls of Shin home Roberto-style. Sanctum was only eighth, so, after picking up my winnings, I took a down-in-the-mouth Dad off for a cup of tea. Now convinced that Curley was the best thing to happen in racing since Sir Gordon Richards, Dad was back on the bandwagon for Nice Guy, and, besides having a £12 10s–£1 between us, I remembered to return to the Tote and exchange my Tote Treble ticket for Paddy Prendergast's horse on leg number two.

The form suggested another Irish challenger, Le Levanstell, had better credentials than Nice Guy, but going to post it was noticeable that our fellow's ribs were sticking out – Curley was right, he was fit to run for his life. Geoff Lewis tried to make all on subsequent Derby fourth Auroy, but Gosling picked him off at the two-furlong pole, and with Joe Mercer also producing Le Levanstell half-way up the straight, Nice Guy needed to dig deep to beat them off and win by half a length and the same.

Cries of 'Curley for Prime Minister' echoed around the tea bar, and, having persuaded Dad that we should miss the fifth and keep our powder dry for Soldanella in the finale, we adjourned to the beer tent and celebrated with a light ale – shandy for yours truly. And who should we meet in the 'Jack Tar' but the bold Curley, who seemed totally oblivious to the fact that he had gone two-thirds of the way to making one schoolboy contemplate retirement even before he had started work! Button-holing Curley, and aided by the shandy, I confidently quizzed him as to how he had come to recommend Soldanella, a horse who had flatly refused to race for Sammy Millbanks in her previous race. Somewhat surprised to be confronted by such a cocky young whipper-snapper, Curley took one step backwards before, realizing that he was attracting an audience again, he said: 'OK son, I'll give you this information free. I heard Lester enquire about the train times to Waterloo – he told this guy he had to stay for the last and that he would win.'

That was good enough for me. It was back to the tatty building behind the bookies to exchange the Tote Treble ticket – the last leg, of course, had to be Soldanella. And Dad, not content with merely cheering on his 'currant bun', stopped off at Nobby's on the way over and had £40–£2: a bet which caused the old guy to choke on his false 'hampsteads'.

Too nervous this time to go down to the gate, we wriggle through the masses to get as close to the winning post as possible. Listening to every word from the racecourse commentator, we chew our finger nails as Soldanella is settled in fourth, then Lester moves her up a place and on the home turn the filly goes second behind Jimmy Lindley on Raymoss. Nearing the furlong pole Lester goes for the gloves, and even trainer Atty Corbett must have been surprised to see her rocket four lengths clear. Raymoss faded and, though Joe Mercer came late on the 7–4 favourite Dusky Prince, it was (thank God) far too late – and Soldanella, who ironically never won again in seven races, had ensured that one red-haired rascal was bitten by the racing bug.

While waiting patiently for the Tote Treble dividend, we called in to see Nobby, who politely handed Dad his 42 smackers and asked us to go in the Silver Ring next time, adding that, but for that bet, him and Florrie would have signed off with a 'skinner'.

Most of the other bookies were smiling, and, while three of the six favourites had obliged, Falls of Shin, Nice Guy and Soldanella had kept the satchels topped up to the brim. There weren't many queuing at the Tote either, but neither of us had a clue as to how much more the Treble might pay.

'Can you take a cheque?' we were asked when the windows eventually opened.

We didn't even have a bank account between us, but we said yes and were greeted by the manager who presented us with a 'kite' for £1,274 5s. All for five bob.

Cycling back through Sunbury and Hanworth (well, we couldn't leave the bikes behind, could we?), it was hard to accept that we had won so much money. My Dad was on a basic wage of £750 per year, so, in one hit, he had mopped up more than eighteen months' earnings.

At the next Kempton meeting we bought Curley a drink, and he confided in us that we had purchased his 'lucky envelope'. Had he given us three duff tips, I would probably have become disillusioned and never have made racing my career.

Some twenty-seven years later I took my own son racing for the first time. We also chose Kempton, though by car, not bikes, and he too made a handsome profit. Here we go again . . .

Geoff Lester joined the Sporting Life *as a messenger boy in 1964. He encountered, touch wood, more ladders than snakes and, having worked through the ranks, he became chief outside reporter in 1985 and received the Lord Derby Award for Journalism in 1988.*

John McCririck
DESSIE AND DISGRACE AT CHELTENHAM

Caution is thrown to the winds at the Cheltenham Festival. The betting rings are hotbeds of frenzy, with an atmosphere so heady that normal judgements simply don't apply. The wheeling and dealing, the scheming and plotting which form the heart of the fascinating world of betting, are here seen at their most fast and furious. It's not just the punters. Bookmakers, too, enter into the reckless spirit of the year's greatest meeting, madly laying bets that would normally be halved or 'bluffed' (not accepted). Two memories – one glorious, the other recalled with shame – stand out from decades of prowling round the jungle of the Prestbury Park rings.

So many Cheltenham occasions glow in the recollection, so many heroes (and heroines) have kept their appointments with destiny up that grinding hill. Arkle, Persian War, Night Nurse (who on the day of the 1977 Champion Hurdle drifted from 5–2 to 15–2 before beating Monksfield and Dramatist), Sea Pigeon, Dawn Run – all wove their way into the magical tapestry of Cheltenham. But Desert Orchid – the whole nation's beloved Dessie – not only raised the grandstand roof when battling back to pass the gallant Yahoo on the run-in, he put the icing on the cake by rubbing those bookie chappies' noses deep into the Cheltenham mud.

Bookies fell over themselves to lay Dessie. In handicaps he had big weights, and in the championship races he often looked vulnerable, especially at Cheltenham. Before the 1989 Gold Cup the grey had run five times at the course, and never won. It was widely accepted that he disliked left-handed courses – he'd won only one steeplechase going that way round, the Chivas Regal Cup at Liverpool in April 1988. But what really seemed to have put paid to his chance in the 1989 Gold Cup was the rain and snow which transformed the going to heavy – conditions Dessie was known to hate.

The nation may have been willing him on, but for the unsentimental bookmakers here was a golden opportunity to 'get' the horse. Convinced that he couldn't win, they pushed his price out from 'face' (5–2) to 'carpet and a half' (7–2), and stood him for their maximum as punters waded in – almost literally on that sodden Thursday afternoon! – to express their loyalty. All around me I witnessed the surge of punters putting their money where their hearts were and driving Dessie's price down to 5–2 SP. One panicking clerk was madly screaming to his guv'nor, 'Go 9–4, you're well over with it!' Rails bookmaker Colin Webster laid £36,000 to £12,000, and after the race lamented: 'He's cost us a fortune this year, and today was by far the worst.'

But for thousands of racegoers in Tatts there was only the vaguest idea of the drama being played out as Yahoo led Dessie towards the second last fence. 'Mushes' (umbrellas), some of them two deep on the rails, obscured the course, and pandemonium from the stands as Dessie collared Yahoo drowned out course commentator Raleigh 'Bwana' Gilbert. Still, whether we could see or not, it was all too gloriously obvious that Dessie had done it, and as the clamour eventually died down it was calculated that his victory had taken over £250,000 out of the ring.

But don't cry too hard for the bookies. On the same day the *Daily Express* Triumph Hurdle went to Ikdam at 'double double carpet' (66–1), and in the last odds-on Rusch de Farges was the vehicle for what was reckoned to be the largest individual losing on-course bet ever seen – £40,000 to £90,000! Talk about the Getting Out Stakes! And not many punters did get out, the race going to the complete 'rag', 66–1 shot Observer Corps.

A much more inglorious memory of Cheltenham in March goes back to my initial involvement with bookmaking there. It was Gold Cup day again, 1969, and I was way out in the centre of the course. Despite pretty juicy results for the books on the opening days, Persian War's second of three Champion Hurdles on the Wednesday knocked out a 'sticker-in' (partner) in a small firm of fiddlers (bookmakers for whom a bet bigger than a pony (£25) was almost unheard of – unless the tic-tacs were showing a bigger price elsewhere!). Somehow, along with a couple of pals, I got roped in as a substitute shareholder. Between the three of us we scraped together our 'case' (last) £300, making the firm's tank for the day a healthy-looking monkey (£500) after exes.

Details of the early races are hazy. But I know that Specify, who went on to win the Grand National two years later, was no good in the opener; Coral Diver's Triumph Hurdle further depleted funds, and by the time we came to the last having unluckily caught a score (£20) each-way the outsider Gay Knight in the County Hurdle, the tank had leaked so badly that it was dry.

There were two options: the honourable one of packing up and creeping disconsolately home, or the other one, attempting to smash our way out of trouble. Unfortunately the necessary funds were not on hand to pursue the bolder course, and our firm's credit-worthiness with the tic-tacs was non-existent. This was when that irrational Cheltenham madness took over and it is with shame that my small part in the sorry affair is recounted.

Virtually 'potless', we nevertheless went to work on the Foxhunters, the final contest of that year's meeting. There were ten runners and the day's banker – indeed, the shortest-priced horse at the whole fixture – was the Welsh champion Battle Royal, winner of his three hunter chases the previous season. On his reappearance at Wincanton three weeks before Cheltenham he had comfortably accounted for a leading rival, Highworth, who was to win the Foxhunters twelve months later. At an ill-tempered, hastily convened conference of desperate partners behind the joint, I went along with the ignoble scheme insisting only that no horse, apart from the favourite, was to be laid. Everything else was running for us including Branch Office, a distant fourth behind that afternoon's Gold Cup hero What A Myth at Newbury earlier in the month. Scraping together a few quid, I sneaked about nicking a pound here, £50–£3 and £50–£3½ there, on the beast (partnered by John Lawrence, now the Noble Lord, John Oaksey) at 20–1, 100–6 and 100–7. Meanwhile the firm, not requiring the services of a hitherto useless floorman to take on all-comers over Battle Royal, got going into him. When generally offered at evens, we went 11–10; at 5–4, our price was 11–8; and, although the form-book doesn't mention it, we in fact laid 6–4 the returned 11–8 chance. It took up two columns in our field book and in all we stood Battle Royal to lose nearly £800 – a fair sum even now but twenty years ago a princely amount, especially in the cheap ring.

The weather was as appalling as on Dessie's day, the going atrocious and race-reading, at least from our lowly pitch, impossible. With the commentary virtually unintelligible over the crackling loudspeakers, only odd glimpses of the runners or snatches of sound gave us any clue as to what was going on. However, whenever news filtered through of Branch Office it proved discouraging. He seemed always to be at the back and Chaseform's 'not jump well, last when blundered 22nd, pulled up before 24th' sums it up. (I must remember to ask the Noble Lord why he didn't persevere.) As for Battle Royal, he always appeared to be lobbing along ready to produce his renowned turn of foot. Coming down the hill at least half the field had gone, and approaching the last the 10–1 chance Queen's Guide was our only hope. Somehow he cleared the final fence and agonizingly, as Battle Royal weakened, arrived at the winning post almost in slow motion, an official twenty lengths clear of the exhausted 'bogey' (biggest loser).

It is without pride that I relate our exultant cheers of sheer relief were embarrassingly loud and prolonged. But, with borrowing the necessary from colleagues not feasible, what would have happened had Queen's Guide fallen? Punters getting out of trouble in the last, and workmen who had taken advantage of our unusual generosity, were not likely to take kindly to being asked to leave their names and addresses for payment by cheque in the post. And the slight problem of somehow raising £800 between us hadn't even been considered in the pre-race confusion. Ever since that unhappy day I've had my suspicions whenever a layer takes on the ring over one short-priced horse. Either he knows something detrimental about the animal's prospects that the rest of us don't. Or it will be a 'names and addresses' job.

You have been warned.

John McCririck filled various roles for course bookmakers and was a private handicapper before becoming a journalist. He worked on the Sporting Life *from 1972 until 1984 and is now At Large in the* Racing Post. *He has been with Channel Four Racing since 1983, and is the author of* John McCririck's World of Betting. *In 1991 he was nominated one of the Fifty Best-Dressed Men in Britain.*

John Hislop
TWO COUPS FROM CLAREHAVEN

My first tale concerns a horse called Baydon, a bay colt foaled in 1919, bred and owned by Lord Wavertree, who later gave his stud to the nation.

Wavertree was an unusual, somewhat eccentric character. Born on Christmas Day, 1856, he was educated at Harrow, where he proved a gifted games player. From Harrow he entered the family brewing business which, however, does not appear to have preoccupied him, since he took an active part in civil affairs, was a Member of Parliament, joined the Volunteers, becoming a colonel, and achieved much success in racing, training and riding ponies, a sport popular in those days and separate from racing under Jockey Club and NH Rules. He was a keen hunting man and owned the Grand National winner of 1896, The Soarer.

In the early years of the twentieth century Wavertree began to take an interest in Flat racing and breeding, founding his stud at Tully, near Kildare. Though wealthy, Wavertree was careful with money and never gave high prices for horses. Despite this he achieved outstanding success as a breeder and owner, heading the lists on more than one occasion and breeding many Classic winners, the best of them being Prince Palatine, whom he nevertheless sold, it is said, because of an adverse horoscope. Wavertree was a firm believer in astrology, and made no decision on racing or breeding without reference to the portents offered by the stars.

Difficult to work for, he held firm views on training and riding, often changed trainers, and had in him a devious streak. This was evident in his management of Night Hawk. He instructed his trainer, Robinson, specifically to prepare the horse for the Cesarewitch, then suddenly ordered it to be sent to Doncaster for the St Leger. Robinson objected that the horse was not fit enough

39

but, as Wavertree later said: 'I knew the colt required very little work and expected him to win. In order to have the laugh over Robinson I put £50 on for him without telling him. To my utter surprise I got 50–1 to the money.' Night Hawk won.

In 1915 Wavertree virtually retired from racing and breeding. The reasons given for this move were that had Cherry Lass been ridden with better judgement she would have won the St Leger, instead of finishing third to Challacombe and Polymelus; and on account of Let Fly running in the Two Thousand Guineas without shoes, though the night before Wavertree had selected the plates he was to wear; also because his instructions as to how Let Fly was to be ridden in the Derby, in which he finished second to Pommern, were disobeyed. However, as the *Bloodstock Breeders Review* stated in Wavertree's obituary, a more probable explanation for Let Fly's failure is that the colt was feeling the effects of a series of gruelling races the previous year with Redfern, who suffered the same way.

After disposing of his stud to the nation, Wavertree only kept an odd horse or two in training. These, true to their owner's principles, were either cheaply acquired or unfashionably bred. Baydon was one of these, and the coup eventually planned for him reflected the eccentric and quirkish nature of his owner.

From the records it is not easy to discover where Baydon was trained at any particular time. At the start of 1922 he was listed as being in Wavertree's private stable, under the charge of Jock Fergusson, who looked after his employer's racing interests in general – or thought he did – and trained the horses in the home stable. Nevertheless the three maiden races won by Baydon that year are attributed in the form-book to Dobson Peacock of Middleham. In 1923 Baydon was listed as trained by Fergusson, for whom he ran last in a mile handicap at Haydock and a five-furlong handicap at Liverpool on, respectively, 20 and 26 July. Then he disappeared from Fergusson's yard for an unknown destination.

Shortly after Baydon ran at Haydock, the formidable Peter Purcell Gilpin instructed his head lad at Clarehaven to send to Newmarket station to meet a hunter consigned to his son, Victor, have it led back to Clarehaven and delivered to the hack stables. This was nothing unusual; Victor often dealt in hunters, buying them in the summer, getting them fit by hacking them on the Heath and either passing them on at the end of the hunting season, or, if he was offered a good enough profit, selling them beforehand. The horses in the hack stables were fed the same oats and hay as the racehorses, to ensure that all the forage on the place was of equally high standard.

In due course the horse arrived; a bay with a hogged mane, a good sort but with nothing to distinguish him from a decent, run-of-the-mill, lightweight hunter. Victor rode him out with the string daily, giving him plenty of work in doing so, and the horse thrived on it. After a couple of weeks, Gilpin senior remarked to the head lad: 'The horse that's been working with the two-year-olds since the spring looks as if he could do with a bit of a rest. That new horse that Mr Victor bought the other day seems a hardy sort with a bit of quality about him; move him over to the racing yard and he can work with the two-year-olds till the other horse is freshened up again.'

This was done, and the hunter proved able to do the job well, being a good mover with a surprising turn of foot even for a well-bred lightweight hunter.

About 18 September Victor informed the head lad that he had sold the hunter, with the agreement of his father, as the other lead horse was refreshed and in action again; and gave instructions for the horse to be put on a train at Newmarket, consigned to a Mr Smith at Peterborough, where he would be met. So far as the lads at Clarehaven were concerned, that was the last of this horse. At Peterborough he was met by Wavertree's travelling lad and taken to a stable at Ayr, arriving the day before the Gold Cup, in which Wavertree had entered Baydon. Victor's 'hunter' and Baydon were, of course, one and the same horse.

In those days there was no overnight declaration of horses; the press had to find out the runners and riders as best they could, and until the declaration of runners forty-five minutes before the advertised time of the race, no accurate list of runners and riders was available. Baydon, who was set to carry 7st 2lb, was down as being trained by Fergusson, but press enquiries to the latter only received the reply that the horse had left his stable in July and he had no idea where he was. No jockey of note had been engaged to ride Baydon, so he was generally supposed to be a non-runner.

When the runners for the Gold Cup went up in the frame, Baydon appeared as ridden by an obscure jockey called Stanton, who had been engaged to ride at Ayr that day with the instruction that he would be told the race for which he was required when he got there.

Starting at 100–6, Baydon won by two lengths from Poetaster, a three-year-old carrying 7st 9lb, bringing off a substantial gamble.

Baydon returned to Clarehaven, from where he won his next race, the October Handicap at Haydock; but no one knew that it was from the Clarehaven stable that he was sent out to win the Ayr Gold Cup. In the records he is shown as having been trained for the race by Fergusson.

Lord Wavertree's penchant for an occasional well planned coup never deserted him. In 1931, the year I went to Clarehaven, when Victor Gilpin was in charge, he sent us a home-bred two-year-old filly, Mitch, by Great Surprise out of Vonna; a nice, neat little individual, she was moderate, but showed enough ability to be fairly certain of winning a selling race at a minor meeting. Victor Gilpin informed Wavertree of this and was told to proceed with the plan to have a touch with her in a race of this type.

Communications with Wavertree were usually made through Jock Fergusson, who therefore was aware of the plan devised for Mitch. The relationship between Wavertree and Fergusson must have been an odd one, since the former said to Victor: 'When you loose the filly, don't say anything to Fergusson about it,' and the latter remarked to Victor: 'We'll have this one to ourselves, so don't let the old man know when she's off.' I don't know how Victor reacted, but suspect that Fergusson was the one left in the dark.

True to the somewhat devious methods which amused Wavertree, Mitch was given a preliminary race in a seller at Folkstone, in which she started at 100–6 and finished out of the first six. Just over a month later she was entered in a similar race at Pontefract, where the class could reasonably be expected to be lower. Meanwhile she had worked well enough for the lads in the yard and local touts to realize that she should be a reasonably good thing in a moderate seller; thus it became necessary to 'take the taste out of their mouths', in order to get a good price on the day. So the trial ground on the racecourse side was booked, which had to be done overnight and meant that every tout in Newmarket, as well as all the Clarehaven lads, knew that something was up. A field of four or five, including Mitch, was named, the riders had colours up and all was set for the trial. Mitch was ridden by a reliable lad called Arthur Crickmere, who was told to finish last and keep his mouth shut and was assured that he would be on the odds when Mitch ran.

Everything worked to plan. Mitch, last in the trial, was sent to Pontefract; Victor took our secretary, Douglas Meacock, and me shooting in the depths of Suffolk to ensure there was no leakage from us; the money was placed SP and Mitch won comfortably at 6–1. She was sold after the race and never won again.

I suspect that the operation amused Wavertree as much as some of his Classic victories.

John Hislop, a former racing correspondent of the Observer, *was assistant trainer to Victor Gilpin at Clarehaven and Michel Grove. A successful amateur rider on the Flat and under NH Rules, he is the author of several books and is a member of the Jockey Club.*

Hacking up

Tony Morris
A WORD FROM THE WISE

Bags of self-confidence, even a touch of arrogance – that's what a young reporter needs in order to advance in his profession. I know it's true, because I've seen so much of it; it's the flash fellows, all swagger and bluster, behaving from their first minute in the job as though they've been around for years, who get noticed and get on. With that incontrovertible fact in mind, I wonder now how it is that I've spent my entire working life as a journalist.

Within a few days of my becoming a racing journalist, straight from school at the age of 18, I really wasn't sure I wanted to be one any longer. As I'd been able to write passable essays and had been mad about racing for years, I'd taken it for granted that I was to be the next Clive Graham. The rude awakening as to just what racing journalism entailed, on the bottom rung of the ladder, drained every drop of confidence from me, and went some way towards persuading me that the whole idea had been a dreadful mistake.

I stuck it out for no better reason than that there was no alternative; just to find an alternative would have required nerve, initiative and self-confidence. Devoid of any of those qualities, all I could do was sit around and watch how my elders and betters coped, just occasionally daring to hope that one day something would rub off and I might begin to consider myself one of the team. I was never going to be the eager type, angling for opportunities; on the contrary, I dreaded the prospect of being handed responsibility.

But I couldn't avoid it for ever. Within a month of my arrival on the Press Association's racing desk I was sent out of town to cover a story on my own. The occasion was about as trivial as it could be, but I was over-awed anyway. Maybe the fact that the trip entailed my staying overnight in an hotel (which I had never done before) contributed to my nervous state; I certainly made a complete hash of the task I'd been set.

The disaster did not go unnoticed by my editor, who nevertheless, and for reasons best known to himself, chose not to suggest that I might be more suitably employed elsewhere. He did, though, ensure that I was sent on no further assignments by myself. On the next few occasions when I was let loose from the office, it was ostensibly to act as 'feed' (assistant) to the firm's senior racecourse reporter, but in reality the idea was mainly to let me see how an experienced journalist went about his business. The very idea that anyone as green as I could actually help our number one reporter was ridiculous, and it did not take long to prove that point.

It would not be too difficult to name the day of that particular disaster, but to do so would seem something less than gallant, as it would involve the precise revelation of a lady's age. So I shall say just that the occasion was a day on the Rowley Mile course at Newmarket, with the youthful and useless Morris tagging along behind mentor Dai Davies, who knew absolutely everyone in racing and could not take more than a stride or two without exchanging greetings with someone or other.

Dai tended to guard his contacts jealously, like the old pro he was, so introductions were few and far between; more often he would name people as we walked away from them, along with some terse judgement of their prowess or character which he doubtless expected me to forget. As it happened, the one useful quality of a good journalist which I did possess was a retentive memory, so I probably learnt more than Dai imagined he was imparting. In that respect the exercise was more than worthwhile.

In addition, I could feel safe with Dai, as it was well known that his pride in his job was such that he would not risk delegating any part of it to a raw and ignorant upstart. At least that was what I thought until our progress towards the press stand was halted for the umpteenth time as yet another figure, unknown to me, engaged Dai in conversation. Imagine my horror when Dai turned to me and informed me that, as he had to phone the office immediately, I would have to follow up the story he'd just been given. The word was that Susan Piggott had produced her second child, and the obvious person to confirm the news was the guy we had just seen standing outside the weighing room. I wanted to say: 'What, me?

Speak to Lester Piggott?' But I didn't dare. I was supposed to be a racing journalist, and I was being given the chance to gather the first news of a story that would hit tomorrow's front pages.

'Go to it, laddie, and meet me back in the phone box with a quote,' said Dai, as he sent me on my way. I ran, terrified at the prospect of having to confront a god, perhaps even more terrified at the thought that once again I would demonstrate my inadequacy. What if the god had vanished? Dare I summon him from the weighing room? But my worst fears were allayed; Lester was still standing just where he had been, quite alone and – in theory – approachable.

I approached. Haltingly, I introduced myself, trying to sound composed and not to seem intrusive, failing hopelessly on both counts. 'I understand that Susan has had the baby,' I ventured, offering the query as fact. A few seconds' silence elapsed, a few seconds in which the maestro probably thought that his private life was no bloody business of a young tyro like me. His reply, at any rate, was: 'If she has, it's the first I've heard of it.' I mumbled some feeble apology about obviously having been misinformed, excused myself and darted back for my rendezvous with Dai.

The chief reporter was standing phone in hand as I burst in with the news, or rather non-news. 'It's not true,' I exclaimed, proceeding to relate the conversation I had had with the avowed still-expectant father, hoping for a word of praise for my efforts. I might not have got a story, but at least I had established the truth, hadn't I? Well, actually, no, I hadn't.

'If that's what he told you, he lied,' said Dai. My chin must have hit the floor as he went on: 'I just bumped into Lester's brother-in-law, who told me that Susan has definitely produced a second daughter, and I have already dictated the story.'

Did Dai believe I had spoken to Lester? I shall never know. But he must have thought that I was either a liar myself, or daft enough not to recognize a lie when I heard one. I can only assume that he did not send word of this débâcle to the editor, because I heard no more about it and remained on the staff. Spared to pursue my bungling efforts at racing journalism, I learnt at least one lesson from that distressing episode. I wouldn't waste my time trying to read Lester Piggott's mind. Whether the idol of my youth had been malicious or merely mischievous in telling me a bare-faced lie at our first meeting was neither here nor there. I was just grateful that his action had not ended my career at a stroke, as it might have done, and I at least knew that I could feel free to disbelieve anything he might say to me in the future.

It was not so very long afterwards that I was able to exercise my cynicism where the great L. Piggott was concerned. And as I could employ it without further risk to my livelihood, it pleased me to do so. On that occasion I counted the cost in a different way.

I had escaped from the office again, on a day trip to Leicester with another of the PA's senior reporters, Geoff Mayes. As was our wont, we ambled around the enclosures before racing began in the vague hope that a chance meeting might provide a little usable information, either for the firm's or our own personal benefit. And to the surprise of neither of us, we wound up outside the weighing room as ignorant as when we'd set out from the press room. As we stood there idly, gazing on a scene of total racecourse ordinariness, out popped the maestro, looking about as bored as we were.

'Let's have a word with Lester,' said Geoff. 'For what it's worth,' I mumbled disparagingly, without going into the details of my previous encounter. 'Lester's all right, once you get to know him,' my colleague assured me. 'Great sense of humour.' I grunted, and maintained a distant second place as we sidled over to where the great man stood. There was a 'hello' from Geoff and a nod of recognition from Lester; I held back, refusing to allow my idolatry of the riding genius to take over from my contempt over the humiliation he had caused me. I declined to speak and offer him the opportunity to deceive me again – but I couldn't help listening to what passed between him and my partner.

'I should think you'll have a good day today,' Geoff chanced, and swift as a flash the rejoinder was: 'I'll win on four.' Such openness was, to say the least, unexpected, even by my colleague, and the pair of us tried to seem nonchalant as we fumbled through our racecards, wondering how best to translate its dull statement of six Piggott rides into the supposed revelation of four Piggott winners. With his eye to the main chance, and perhaps more reason than I had to give Lester credence, Geoff sallied forth. 'Well, Costmary's a certainty in the last,' he suggested, winning a nod of assent. 'And I suppose Chiltern Miss might win the maiden, if she can beat Pristina,' my colleague continued. 'I'll beat her all right,' the maestro replied. And so it went on. 'Well, you're not going to win the first, because Jack Jarvis's is a certainty.' Body language, rather than words, conveyed confirmation of that assertion. 'What about the seller? You'll never give the weight to Carson's mount, will you?' 'I'll beat that, no trouble,' was the matter-of-fact answer.

We were nearly there, and Geoff seized the initiative. 'Well, the old man's horse, Extortion, that must be the other one,' he ventured. Lester shook his head. 'Not to be trusted, that b*gg*r,' was the verdict on this obvious favourite, and by now I was more than ever convinced that the press were again being led astray. Piggott was a fine one to talk about trust, I thought, and apparent confirmation of my scepticism followed immediately. 'Well, that only leaves Seymour, and he's a dodgier character than Extortion these days,' said Geoff, with all the justification that any self-respecting journalist with a thorough knowledge of the form-book could muster. 'I'll win on Seymour,' said Lester defiantly, adding outrageously, 'and if I don't finish first, I'll get it in the Stewards' room.'

The man was beyond redemption. It was one thing to take advantage of an unknown cub reporter on what might just have been construed as an intrusive errand, but it was something else again to dole out to the press the sort of duff information which invited contempt and ridicule.

I didn't go near the betting ring that day. I wasn't tempted after the fulfilment of the first-race prophecy, when the Jarvis horse won as he liked, nor after the seller, in which Piggott conjured a second run out of Held Firm to floor the lightly weighted Carson mount Brebner, nor even after the third, in which Extortion started at odds-on and ran with all the unwillingness his partner had predicted.

But it was the fourth which finally convinced me that I was a born loser. Seymour was never going well enough to win it, and was clearly – if narrowly – beaten by a better horse at the weights. But as the struggle developed in the final furlong, this horse, who habitually found trouble or made it for himself, was made to look unlucky. Realizing that he could win nothing from the judge or from the camera, his rider determined to catch the attention of the Stewards, putting on a display of histrionics worthy of Hollywood. The difference was that it was a performance not captured on celluloid; the era of the camera patrol had not arrived. The only image available to the Stewards was the brief recall of a horse suddenly snatched up, as though impeded, reinforced at the subsequent inquiry by his rider's convincing plea of injured innocence. A panel of two well informed pressmen might have decreed otherwise, but the verdict rested with three unenlightened Stewards, who promptly reversed the placings of the first two home.

The afternoon pursued its inevitable course. Pristina gave Chiltern Miss a struggle, but a head verdict went Piggott's way, and the obvious doddle for Costmary (at odds of 8–100) was duly enacted in the last. The Piggott prophecies had proved uncannily accurate, while the state of the Morris exchequer had budged not at all. I resolved that the next time that particular god offered me a glimpse into the future, I would pay more heed. Sadly, I'm still waiting.

Tony Morris is a freelance journalist and author of several books on racing and breeding. As bloodstock correspondent of the Racing Post, *he was named Racing Journalist of the Year in 1990.*

Roger Mortimer
TRAVELLING FORM

At the end of June 1947 I left the Army after seventeen mostly happy if undistinguished years. My last duty was to act as second-in-command at the King's Birthday Parade on Whitehall, an occasion less colourful than usual as we were not yet back to tunics and bearskins. I was mounted on a police horse, a gelding inappropriately named Virile who was extremely well behaved except for a habit of urinating whenever the massed bands struck up *God Save the King*. I remained on friendly terms with Virile and made a point of having a few words whenever I came across him on duty at Epsom or Hurst Park.

Since I was due to get married in the autumn it was clearly advisable to find a job. Ever since my preparatory school days when a glass-eyed usher with a genius for teaching history used to lend me a lively weekly publication called *The Jockey* – the paper's motto was '*The Jockey* is on every winner' – I had been hooked on racing. A former brother-officer of mine called Roger de Wesselow ran a very successful weekly form-book called *Raceform* (*Chaseform* during the winter), as well as a number of other publications connected with the Turf. The most popular of these was a four-page weekly named *The Racehorse*, parts of which were not wholly unreminiscent of that famous late Victorian and Edwardian paper of the Turf and the stage, the *Sporting Times* (far more commonly known as 'The Pink 'Un', from the colour of the paper on which it was printed; at most schools you got into trouble if you were caught reading the Pink 'Un, its particular brand of humour being mildly salacious). Evidently someone somewhere was entertained by my column in *The Racehorse* and out of the blue I was invited to join *The Sunday Times* which at that point of time had no racing correspondent. In fact, *The Sunday Times* was not much concerned with racing. The great Lord Kemsley knew as much about the Turf as the average Eskimo does about county cricket, while the editor was over 80 years of age. (I cannot recollect ever having seen him, let alone having spoken to him.) However, *The Sunday Times* paid me a good deal more money than *Raceform* for considerably less work, despite the fact that I was handicapped by knowing absolutely nothing about journalism and its world, however much I thought I knew about racing.

One of my common tasks during my earlier days of journalism was to go racing and provide comments on how each horse had performed for inclusion in the form-books. Sometimes I found myself lumbered with the paddock comments as well so that I was kept on the hop when there were a lot of runners to contend with. Of course, I was never entrusted with the big meetings like Ascot, Epsom, Newmarket, Goodwood, York or Doncaster; to start with I was restricted to the more bucolic jumping fixtures such as Newton Abbot, Plumpton, Wye, Devon and Exeter and Buckfastleigh. Some of these meetings have gone up in the world since then, while others have vanished from the fixture list altogether.

At first I was often put under the wing of the late Bob Haines, who was very good at his job and later became a successful commentator. Before the war we had served in the same battalion in Egypt but the rank consciousness of those days, before he obtained a commission in the Essex Regiment, meant that I did not know him at all well. When the 3rd Coldstream was at Alexandria, we both had weekend jobs at the main racecourse, the Sporting Club. There was a lively racing paper published in French. I was a Steward and was quite chuffed when I saw a large photograph in this paper of the Stewards presenting a handsome Gold Cup to a successful owner. I was a good deal less delighted when I read the caption: 'Fellow Sportsmen of Alexandria, the gentlemen in the above photograph are not only highly incompetent, they are also extremely dishonest.' I think only one of these imputations was true. The critic was punished by temporary suspension of his club membership.

One of the biggest differences between racing now and in the immediate post-war years lies in the travelling. There was no question then of jumping into a fast and reasonably reliable car and pelting down a motorway. Motorways did not exist; not many people owned a car; new ones were virtually unobtainable; and in any case petrol was strictly rationed. By and large racegoers had to rely on the train service, which varied in quality: the best trains were extremely good and the meals offered were far superior to those dished out today. (One line to the north boasted a truly excellent claret at a far from exorbitant price.) The trouble was that at certain times, in the holiday season for instance, trains were in short supply and long journeys perched on a suitcase in the corridor were by no means rare.

For a budding journalist, a life that involved spending so much time in trains had the advantage that one got to know the personalities of the racing world far more quickly than is possible today. Also, there were good parties at certain hotels for the major meetings. Of course if you were not one of the swells you had to watch expenses. I think *Raceform* allowed £2 10s for a night away from home. I found the racing regulars friendly and helpful, not least the Press Association team who journeyed from meeting to meeting and whose knowledge of travelling form was unbeatable. Moreover, they were on excellent terms with those railway officials who could make life easier on a train, not least in a restaurant-car after a crowded meeting.

Metropolitan racegoers were well looked after by the railway companies and a run-of-the-mill afternoon at Hurst Park not only catered adequately for the general public but also provided special trains for first-class passengers and members of the Club where racing was taking place. On one occasion, going to Hurst Park in a first-class-only train, I shared a compartment with two colonels from the Cavalry Club and their ladies. Just as the train was moving out of Waterloo a tipster called Healy, who always wore an old Harrovian tie, evaded the watchful attendants on the platform and joined us. The colonels regarded him with some suspicion but he gave no trouble and was soon immersed in the *Sporting Life*. The journey was nearly over when he laid down his paper and addressed his fellow-passengers. 'Ladies and gentlemen,' he stated in ringing tones, 'all I can tell you is this. If General Advance don't win today, I'll [remainder of his little speech must be censored].'

I think it was in 1948 that I received a note from *Raceform* warning me for duty at Buckfastleigh on Saturday 7 August. I had never been to Buckfastleigh, which expired not many years later. It formed part of what is known as the Devon circuit and racing had just started there again after the war. All I could discover about it was that it was situated not far from Buckfast Abbey. As I could not locate a hotel close to the racecourse I judged it best to take a train from London to Exeter and play it from there. There was a solitary train to Exeter on the Friday and, it being the height of the holiday season and holidays abroad not being then permitted, the train was crammed. I was lucky to get a pitch in the corridor. Restaurant cars were off.

Exeter is not short of modest hotels of a vaguely ecclesiastical flavour, and not being able to find a cab I humped my bag to one of these. I was unable to detect any form of public transport to the races the following day and I was beginning to get desperate when a hotel porter suggested I approach the cook and arrange terms for the loan of her bicycle. A small amount of money changed hands and I became the temporary possessor of a solid-looking machine which the sporting local auctioneer would doubtless have described as 'absolutely sound, up to fourteen stone, has carried a lady'.

It was a damp, muggy day on the Saturday and there was a lot of pedalling to be done before reaching the racecourse. I started almost at dawn to ensure getting there in time; a bit too early, in fact, as the pay-gates had not been opened when I arrived, although a number of people seemed to have found a way in. Actually, the turnstiles did not start to operate till about an hour before the first contest, at which point a coachload of Devon police arrived, alighted, linked arms and marched through the enclosures, sweeping outside all individuals who had got in without the formality of paying. These intruders were coerced into orderly queues and duly paid up at the turnstiles.

I was surprised at the total lack of anything that looked like a permanent building; their absence, combined with the presence of a row of marquees, suggested a point-to-point rather than a meeting under National Hunt Rules. A notice on the racecard apologized for the somewhat primitive conditions and attributed the lack of a grandstand to shortage of labour. Luckily there was a rise in the ground from which a fair view of the racing could be obtained.

To pass the time I walked round the course, which appeared to be well maintained. The fences were well made; I discovered that they had been constructed by German prisoners-of-war incarcerated in the vicinity. The quality of the sport was better than I had expected and there was a total of close on sixty runners for the six races. The standard of the jockeys riding was high; among those taking part was the late Bryan Marshall, destined to win the Grand National on Early Mist and Royal Tan, both trained by Vincent O'Brien. Oddly enough, in fact, there were three jockeys riding at Buckfastleigh that day who were unlucky *not* to win the Grand National. Lord Mildmay, a loyal supporter of the Devon circuit, would surely have won the 1936 National on his 100–1 outsider Davy Jones, a big entire chestnut, if only his reins had not broken at the penultimate fence. Mildmay was probably equally unlucky in 1948 when third on Cromwell. Owing to a previous shoulder injury suddenly reasserting itself, he was quite unable to help Cromwell at all in the closing stages of the race. Dick Francis, only recently out of the RAF and long before he wrote his first book, was second in the first event at Buckfastleigh, an optional selling hurdle. In the 1956 Grand National, riding the Queen Mother's Devon Loch, he had the race apparently at his mercy when just short of the winning post Devon Loch suddenly collapsed, a mystery that has yet to be conclusively solved.

Cromwell was not the only unlucky competitor in the 1948 Grand National. The 100–1 outsider Zahia, a mare trained by Major Geoffrey Champneys, was ridden by Eddie Reavey who won a chase at Buckfastleigh this very afternoon. Zahia had the National well won coming to the last fence but somehow Reavey contrived to go the wrong way, and that was that.

Also riding at Buckfastleigh that day was Johnny Bullock, late of the airborne forces, who won the 1951 Grand National on the mare Nickel Coin. Amateurs in the saddle included Mr J. Seely, who won the three-mile chase and whose son Mr Michael Seely is today a leading racing journalist, and Captain Roly Beech, a dashing 12th Lancer who had won the MC in North Africa.

I was desperately tired when I got back to Exeter and returned the bicycle that had served me so well. I had quite enjoyed my trip to Devonshire. I was never detailed to go there again.

Roger Mortimer began his career as a regular officer in the Coldstream Guards and turned to racing journalism after the Second World War. He was racing correspondent of the The Sunday Times *for 28 years and wrote many books, including* The History of the Derby Stakes. *He died in November 1991.*

Fred Shawcross
WHEN BAKHAROFF BACKED OFF

Let me recount the tale of how I came to tip the winner of the 1986 Ever Ready Derby, and subsequently bask in the glare of totally undeserved glory.

I was racing editor/columnist of *Today* at the time. The newspaper was in its infancy, struggling for survival against bigger, far more powerful rivals, and we were desperate to score points wherever and whenever we could. Finding winners, especially winners of big races, is a tried and tested system of point-scoring.

In the run-up to the 1986 Derby, I had managed to become utterly besotted with a noble animal by the name of Bakharoff, trained by Guy Harwood at Pulborough, in glorious West Sussex. For some reason, which totally escaped me, my colleagues in the media were equally besotted with Bakharoff's stable-companion, a certain Dancing Brave, who had already won the Craven Stakes and Two Thousand Guineas. Bakharoff's pre-Derby programme hadn't produced quite the same encouragement, though I preferred to rely on his triumph in the William Hill Futurity the previous October, his position at the head of the 1985 Two-Year-Old Free Handicap and the (for me) inescapable fact that he would be better the further he had to travel.

In the last anxious weeks before the great day, I held unswerving to my belief that Bakharoff would win the Derby, despite equally strong views expressed in other quarters that Mr Harwood would choose to rely on Dancing Brave as his stable number one, with Allez Milord number two and Bakharoff reduced to the role of spectator before being re-routed to Chantilly for the French Derby, the following Sunday. I had checked with the ever- helpful Mr Harwood, of course, but he insisted that no decision would be made until the last minute. I concluded that all three would run

– a decision which, in history, will rank with Napoleon's decision to invade Russia!

The sports editor of *Today* at that time was a volatile Scot called Len Gould, a brilliant journalist but a man not noted for his patience or sympathy with elderly racing scribes with misguided allegiance to Derby contenders. He regularly urged me to rethink my strategy; to abandon Bakharoff in favour of another runner, say Dancing Brave, or at least one certain, barring unforeseen circumstances, actually to go to post. The more he pleaded, then harangued, the more I dug in my heels. It was Bakharoff for me.

I should explain here that what worried the excellent Mr Gould was not merely that he considered Bakharoff a serious no-hoper, but that my Derby preview had to be written forty-eight hours or so in advance of the race to give the production staff of *Today* time to prepare the special Derby Day pull-out. New technology hadn't done a great deal to change the old set-and-hold system; in fact, in my somewhat jaundiced opinion, we had marched steadily backwards.

So there we were, two days before the big race, my thoughts on the Derby in print, waiting for the presses to roll. Under the headline 'It's Bakharoff', and a splendid picture of the colt, were my considered thoughts leading to the conclusion that Bakharoff would beat Dancing Brave and Shahrastani. The dye, as they say, was cast. Now all I had to do was sit back and watch my choice do the business. Some hope.

The day before the great race, I was making my way from my *pied-à-terre* in West Kensington to the *Today* office in Vauxhall Bridge Road. The paper's racing desk in those days was a force of one (me), and I faced the task of reporting the world's greatest Flat race from an armchair in front of the television set in the editor's office. But that wasn't the thought uppermost in my mind as I left Victoria underground station to walk the half-mile or so to the office. I needed to know if Bakharoff was among the overnight declarations for the 1986 Ever Ready Derby. My career – nay, my head – and close to £300 of my hard-earned cash were riding on him. For some reason, I began to sweat as I nudged open the door of the local Mecca betting shop. The manager, a cheerful soul, looked uncharacteristically solemn, a worried look on his normally smiling face. He knew the extent of my involvement with Bakharoff. Like a judge at an Old Bailey trial, he pronounced sentence: 'Sorry, mate. It's a non-runner.'

I was dead. Dead and buried. And what's worse, skint! No; worst of all, I had Len Gould to face. Not a happy prospect. I do not exaggerate when I tell you that the dressing-down I received that morning was possibly the best (or worst, depending upon where one was standing) in newspaper history. Mr Gould lashed me verbally for what seemed hours. 'Incompetent', 'addle-brained', 'senile' were just some of the adjectives hurled in my direction. And they were the most complimentary. In conclusion the Manic Celt informed me that I had around two minutes to rewrite my Derby preview and change the headline and picture.

No problem to someone facing the firing squad. I legged it down to the picture library and found we had a photograph of Shahrastani which virtually matched that of Bakharoff (Thankyou God). The letters of Shahrastani's name more or less coincided with those of Bakharoff. So a judicious bit of juggling with the typeface on the computer changed 'It's Bakharoff' to 'It's Shahrastani'. Finally, a hasty rewrite convinced my reader(s) that I had all along been in no doubt that the Aga Khan-owned, Michael Stoute-trained, Walter Swinburn-ridden colt would win the Derby.

The rest is history. On Derby Day 1986 I sat in front of editor Brian MacArthur's television and roared home Shahrastani like a dervish, while the rest of the *Today* staff looked on in rapt amazement. What had been the worst period of my professional life suddenly became the best. OK, perhaps Dancing Brave was the unluckiest loser of all time; subsequent events proved he almost certainly was. I cared not a jot. My bacon was saved and the following day the front page of *Today* proudly proclaimed that Fred Shawcross, the nation's number one racing tipster, had named the 11–2 winner of the Derby. Isn't life wonderful?

No, I didn't back him. And fate decided, just in case I thought I'd got the game licked, to deal me a considerable smack in the gob. Convinced that Bakharoff had been switched from Epsom to Chantilly to win the French Derby, I chivvied the long-suffering Mr Gould to underwrite the cost of a trip to France, to report on a confidently expected English victory. Much to my surprise – and his too, I suspect – he agreed and, the following Sunday, I arrived at a sun-drenched Chantilly to cheer home Bakharoff.

Well, he got home . . . but about ten minutes behind the local champion Bering. I lost *beaucoup de francs*, doing even more damage to my shattered finances; Len Gould's opinion that I was incredibly stupid, or seriously mad, was confirmed I was left with just one outlet: to jump in the Seine.

So I did.

Fred Shawcross is editorial director of Satellite Information Services. He has been a journalist for 40 years and been employed as a sportswriter on several national newspapers. He breeds and owns greyhounds and has a share in winning hurdler, Montagnard.

Ian Carnaby
THE ONE THAT GOT AWAY

The telephone does not often startle me at 8 a.m. The fact is, I'm nearly always awake by 7 – not for any particularly virtuous reason, but simply because one's more pressing financial concerns seem slightly easier to bear from a non-horizontal position.

I'd been working for BBC Radio on a *Sport on Four* piece until well after midnight on Friday, and it was about 2 a.m. when I arrived back in Newbury.

'Ian? Ian Carnaby?'

Might as well admit it. 'Speaking.'

'It's Tony Jakobson. Where are you? We're all here waiting. What's going on?'

Not an easy question to answer, especially stark naked on a cold March morning. Let me put my side of it first.

As far as I was concerned, Tony (the long-serving Newmarket correspondent of the *Sporting Life*) was organizing a weekend trip to Cyprus for a group of British journalists. A jockeys' challenge match had been arranged against the Greek Cypriots, with the 'away' team comprising Steve Cauthen, Pat Eddery, Yves Saint-Martin and Christy Roche. Tony had kindly invited me because the organizers were very keen that a BBC man should attend. I had explained that my workload that particular weekend more or less ruled it out, but if a miracle happened I'd join them at the airport. As he'd made a block booking I thought no further contact was necessary. The *Sport on Four* piece knocked out everything else on the Friday evening, and I'd thought of them all flying out as I put it together.

'Look. I'm at the Hilton in Nicosia and I'm in a real jam. We had you paged at the airport last night and again at the hotel. You've simply got to come. I've promised them the BBC will be here and you've got to fly out. Just ring up and change the ticket and go to Heathrow. Please.'

I've always thought of my inability to say 'no' as the sign of a generous spirit and a readiness to take life on the chin. My wife, however, assures me it's because I'm weak-willed. Mercifully, she and the children were away for the weekend.

'Tony, I can't do that,' I said feebly.

'You can. You must. We'll see you tonight.'

I suppose I must have washed and shaved. I threw everything in a case and drove back to Broadcasting House. In those days I used to broadcast a review of the week's sporting press in *Sports Report* on Radio Two. I'd photocopied a few articles but, of course, there was nothing on paper. It was an odd sort of piece. It included a bit about the current craze for dwarf-tossing in Australia and I managed to counterbalance this with an extract from the sublime chapter on village cricket in A. G. Macdonell's wonderful *England, Their England*. Alastair Down would undoubtedly have called it a piece of 'whimsy-whamsy', and he'd have been right, but I was rather fond of it.

It must have taken about four hours to write and record, after which I hurtled back down the M4 to Heathrow. There was a flight to Larnaca at 4 p.m. I remember little of it apart from a bottle of rather heavy Cypriot red, because I fell asleep.

The taxi ride from Larnaca Airport to the Nicosia Hilton is, however, etched more vividly on the mind. The route took us very close to the Turkish border, established following the invasion of the island in 1974. At first I was happy enough that the driver spoke fluent English, but as his tales of bombs and outrages grew ever more lurid, I was relieved to see the lights of the capital.

Ironic applause can be very wounding sometimes. In fact, ironic applause led by Tony Stafford of the *Daily Telegraph* may even have the edge on sarcasm. He and the others were all sitting in a far corner of the hotel lounge and it felt like a long walk. 'Meester Carnabee! Meester Carnabee!' he kept saying. (Apparently one of the hotel staff had been driving people mad by paging me in this way the night before. Most people would forget something like that pretty quickly, but Tony still has no difficulty in calling it instantly to mind if he sees me in the press room at Newbury, Ascot or wherever.) He was accompanied by his wife Gill, and the others in the group were Tony and Genny Jakobson, Mark Popham of the *Life* and Neil Cook and his fiancée (now his wife) Sarah.

'You missed a great day,' said Cook.

'You've missed the jockeys, too, because they've gone to bed. Big day tomorrow,' said Jakobson. I seem to recall that that did not stop us sipping various beverages until well into the small hours. Needless to say, the women had more sense.

I made a great start on the Sunday.

Any relief I felt at not looking foolish in front of the jockeys as well as the press corps evaporated when I mistook Terry Ellis, Pat Eddery's brother-in-law, for Christy Roche. (Never, ever, admit a mistake of this nature to a racing journalist. Even more importantly, if you do, never, ever beg him to keep quiet about it.)

As we travelled to Nicosia racecourse there was much jovial speculation about the standard BBC recording equipment. This is known as the UHER. As I am to technology what Bob Monkhouse is to introspection I shall not attempt to describe a typical UHER, beyond saying that it is a heavy, portable tape recorder in a black case, the strap of which soon wears a groove in your shoulder. As the banter continued, the unworthy thought crossed the Carnaby mind that, while this might be a pleasurable day in the sun for some, for one member of the party it promised to be just another day at the office.

Nothing could have been further from the truth. It was, in fact, a magnificent day – and I say this as one who finds it difficult to relax until the work is done. Nicosia racecourse is a small, compact, left-handed dirt track, overlooked by the Kyrenia mountains. Everything to do with the racing is run by the Greek Cypriots, but the Turks have established themselves in the mountains and the red flags fly there.

The racing was of a modest standard, but it was keenly contested. It soon became clear why Alias Smith needed an alias. He'd covered enough mares to keep the sport going off his own bat, but typically his sons (eight-year-old geldings, some of them) ran on with great gameness.

There was never any doubt about which team would win the Jockeys' Challenge. While the other three obviously regarded the outing as something of a busman's holiday, Yves Saint-Martin was more inclined to view it as a mixture of Arc day and the Washington International. He could probably have won on Alias Smith.

I began to feel optimistic. The piece, when put together, promised to make an excellent Radio 4 item. It had all the right ingredients: the novelty of a race commentary in Greek, the background effects, and interviews with Panayotis Kazamias, the general manager of the racecourse, and Athos Christodoulou. Athos was deeply committed to racing in Cyprus and, of course, later had the York International winner Ile de Chypre in training with Guy Harwood in England. I recorded my introduction out in the centre of the course, and it only remained to have a little of Steve Cauthen on tape as well. I planned to ask him back at the hotel.

I was even able to devote some attention to the last race, in which I put the remainder of my local money on a horse called Professor. His was the only name I recognized on the commentary and for quite a while it was the only name which mattered, but naturally something came out of the pack to do him on the line.

That evening there was a banquet at which we were sumptuously wined and dined. I made a small mistake here, because had I brought the UHER down from my room I could have recorded Yves when he stood up to make a little speech. As things turned out, Steve preferred to record his piece at the airport the following morning, because after dinner he and the others were going off to a special function in their honour. Once again we sat up until the early hours, and there were some pretty bleary-eyed journalists who boarded the plane. I thought I could have the piece edited and ready by Thursday, in plenty of time for Saturday's *Sport on Four*. It was the happiest I'd seen Tony Jakobson for quite some time.

You will have guessed by now that there is no happy ending to all of this. At first I thought the thunderstruck look on my wife's face was engendered by envy. Foolish mortal. On reflection, it was pretty silly of me to leave the garage doors wide open and the milk on the step. They'd been through every room, and although the police recovered most of our possessions a gold ingot on a chain was lost for ever. Nothing that I've done since has surprised her.

It was a relief to go back to the office. I cannot edit tape, but the studio manager who helped put the piece together was suitably impressed. 'It's different,' he said. Believe me, from a BBC SM this is some compliment.

You're thinking that nothing could have gone wrong after that, but then, you haven't met the producer Emily McMahon. Gifted, moody, imaginative, obsessive, fiercely independent, that sort of thing. We must have worked together on a hundred items.

'I've done the Cyprus thing,' I said.

'Mm?'

'Cyprus. It's done. Six minutes. Finishes up with Steve Cauthen.'

Removes headphones. Slightly glazed look. 'You can't be on twice.'

'Eh?'

Flash of impatience. (It doesn't take much.)

'I said you can't be on twice. I need you to do this Rugby League interview. *Up and Under*. It's a play opening in the West End next week. I've said you'll go down for the rehearsals tonight. Fortune Theatre.'

Heart-beat quickens. 'Ah. Actually this Cyprus piece really is quite good. Did you know you can see the Turkish flags from the course?'

From impatience to anger. I marvel we achieved as much as we did over the years.

'I didn't actually *ask* you to go to Cyprus, Carners.'

Don't panic, and above all don't argue. 'Can it go on next week?'

'I don't see why not.' No, but we both knew a reason would appear as if by magic. (Darts, as I recall.) I didn't want to ring Tony Jakobson with a single apology, let alone two of them.

It never saw the light of day. I'm not even sure Emily listened to it, and it was soon out of date. Criminally, I didn't make an extra copy. If I had, a less honest man than Tony would at least have been able to play it to the Cypriots and say that it had been broadcast – a white lie, but a forgivable one. McMahon lives most of her life knee-deep in tapes. Asking her for the original was as pointlessly optimistic as anything can be.

We all laugh about it now, of course, but I was down for quite a while. Then, like everything else, I found myself thinking about it less frequently, and sometimes I think the memory will fade altogether.

That's generally when I bump into Tony Stafford at the races.

Ian Carnaby worked in the wine trade for eight years before becoming a full-time sports writer and broadcaster. He has been with Extel, BBC Radio, the ill-fated London Daily News, *and* Satellite Information Services

Paul Haigh
THE GETTING BACK STAKES

Getting there was just about all right. It was getting back that was more than half the fun. I'd gone, you see, on a ticket that was cheaper than the average, partly because it went by a circuitous and more interesting route: London, Dubai, Kuala Lumpur, Manila or Cebu (where?), depending on availability, and then, at length, the Land of the Rising Sun and (when you thought about the trip back) the occasional sinking feeling.

My memories of the weekend of the 1989 Japan Cup are rather fragmented. I can remember reaching Tokyo late on the night before the race and checking in at the Keio Plaza Hotel, where – just for an example of the technology they think is normal – the lift goes from the ground floor to the thirty-fourth in three seconds without the passenger being conscious of any but the slightest movement. I can remember applying for my credentials from a reception committee whose members clearly did not expect people to arrive alone at ten to midnight. I can remember that they gazed for some time with a fragile belief that bordered on suspicion. Only later did I discover that the only British racing hack they'd seen up till then was McCririck, and that they therefore felt more than slightly dubious about anyone who didn't wear a stripy blazer, didn't dwarf a sumo, and who just complained quietly that he was shattered. When they pointed the camera in order to provide the picture for the pass without which I would probably have been barred from everywhere except, perhaps, the Tokyo toilets, they had to remind me that the likeness would be impaired if I failed to remove the beercan from my lips. (Little did they know.)

Once you were in, though, you were in. The great womb of the Keio Plaza received you and soothed you, and the great machine of the JRA (the Japan Racing Association) swept you up, catered to your every need and fed you *sushi* and other delicacies at regular intervals. This was just as well, because, as I found out when the party was over and the JRA had decided its responsibility for my welfare was over with it, a cup of coffee in the hotel caff cost – wait for it – the yen equivalent of 5.50. That's pounds. Sterling. And it's probably gone up since then.

I can remember staggering down to the cocktail bar that night where I found Brough Scott drinking a giant pink cocktail with a golf umbrella in it. I can remember waking the next morning and the coach drive to the course – a very slow drive because Tokyo seems to be one vast traffic jam even on a Sunday morning. I can remember Fuchu as a place that makes Ascot look like Bangor-on-Dee: one of the world's great temples to sport (and to a few other things as well).

The Japanese concept of a day at the races is rather different from our own. I sometimes think we think of our racing as an endurance test for those who truly love the sport, as a way for devotees to prove their devotion by ordeal. In Japan they think a day at the races should be fun for everybody, even for those who don't much care who wins. So they have pop groups playing (well away from the horses), clowns performing (real ones) and all sorts of fringe entertainments for those members of the family who just come along for the ride. Because the JRA, a branch of government, controls the betting, it is fabulously wealthy by the standards of our racing. Nearly as wealthy – I'm sorry, but I can't resist the dig – as some of our bookmaking firms. So people get in for peanuts and the facilities are of a splendour we would associate with a high-class hotel rather than with a racecourse stand. The result of all this: they regularly get six-figure crowds. On the day of the 1989 Japan Cup the gate was around 160,000.

What I'm trying to indicate is that what a day at Fuchu has in common with, say, a wet Wednesday at the old Wolverhampton, is horses, and that's about all.

The first four races are run in the late morning. Then there's a break for lunch, during which everyone who's brought a picnic unpacks his or her *sushi* and everyone else, including those few foreigners fortunate enough to find themselves recipients of Japanese corporate hospitality, heads for the corporate trough.

During the lunch interval we were entertained by troupes of

68

baton-twirling girls – I remember them – marching to the music of the Japanese Self Defence Force Band. It is a major solecism, by the way, to refer to these musicians as the Army Band. If you do so you are immediately reminded that since 1945 Japan has had no Army: only a Self Defence Force, whose representatives you see before you today. Confused and embarrassed by this social blunder you smile as sweetly as you are capable, then pipe down and eat your *sushi*.

Racing resumes, and preparations begin for the main event. I can remember the parade ring, set well away from the track and directly adjoining the horses' boxes. You reach it by a huge, brightly lit tunnel, through which the horses, when they've paraded, later reach the track. I can remember Oguri Cap, the Japanese champion, winner of twenty-one out of his twenty-five races and around £3 million in prize money. I can remember thinking that Assatis, who'd been bought by a Japanese syndicate, looked magnificent and that an old grey mare from New Zealand called Horlicks looked very ordinary indeed – until they pulled the rug off her and let us see her muscles. Much later, after racing, Paul Cole, who had Ibn Bey in the race, confirmed for me what I'd known already: that I am a lousy judge of a horse's appearance. Assatis, he said, had clearly gone over the top. Ibn Bey too had suffered, he felt, from his journey. Horlicks looked terrific. Oh, well.

I can remember a great fanfare from the Self Defence Force Band, followed by a roar from the 160,000 as they realized the horses were prepared. And then the race itself.

Assatis never showed. Nor did Carroll House, the Arc winner, who'd also been bought to stand in Japan but who'd clearly had enough racing for the year, maybe for his lifetime. Ibn Bey was up there, then dropped back at the entrance to the straight, at which point the old grey mare proved she was at least what she used to be by dashing through on the rail under David Sullivan, the son of her trainer, to take it up two out. Immediately she was challenged by Oguri Cap and the two drew clear to fight it out to the line, where Horlicks, dour and magnificently game, remained a neck in front in spite of the imploring cheers of Oguri Cap's legion fans.

Afterwards I can remember one New Zealander in particular. Hard to forget him. He was six foot ten, weighed 25 stone and made even the least retiring member of the British press contingent look like a garden gnome. I suspect he might have done the same to the great sumo known as The Dump Truck, though I never got to test the theory. Japanese, who are even less used than we are to encountering persons of such physical dimensions, used to stop and look at him in the same way that tourists might stop and look at a mountain, or engineers might look at a particularly fine example of a box girder bridge. For all his size John was a gentle soul and very approachable. When I saw him after the race he was wearing a beatific smile and clutching a full plastic carrier bag.

'What have you got in the bag, John?'

'About seven million yen.'

Then a press conference at which Sullivan senior told us all how he'd got Horlicks ready, and at which her owner wept tears of pure joy. A great party in the Keio Plaza's splendid banqueting room, or more probably in *one* of the Keio Plaza's splendid banqueting rooms. The food wonderful and varied. *Sushi* also available for those who'd become addicted.

The next day a trip to one of the JRA's training centres. Just me and Janet Slade of *Paris-Turf*, and a coach, and three guides, and a reception committee, and a few picnic boxes full of *sushi*. And then it was time to go home.

Getting back. Now there, as I told you, was the difficult bit. Compared with the high-tech luxury of the Keio Plaza, the Philippines – a beautiful country full of beautiful people, but terribly impoverished by a mixture of exploitation, corruption and a very different view of the world from the Japanese – is a scary place. It's scary at the best of times, and late November 1989 was not the best of times in Manila.

Have you heard of Major 'Gringo' Honasan? Nor had I.

How about Juan Ponce Enrile? Or Raoul Mangalapus? Well, never mind. What about Cory Aquino, the lady who took over the presidency from Marcos, the man who was married to the woman with 3,000 pairs of shoes and only one pair of feet? All come flooding back now, eh?

Well, the problem at the end of November 1989 was that 'Gringo' decided to stage an army coup against Cory, with the connivance, some thought, of Juan, and it was up to Raoul and his friends, I think, to stop this act. I woke up at 6 a.m. on the next morning to the sound of what I thought were the lights shorting loudly but soon turned out to be machine-gun fire.

70

Gringo and the boys took some barracks. They took the commercial district, which included all the embassies. They took the airport, so there were no flights in or out. Taking advantage of the confusion, the members of the New People's Army, who usually spend their time hiding in the hills, decided to visit town. American servicemen at Subic Bay were ordered to stay on base because one of the NPA's main functions in life is to shoot Americans. Foreigners who might be mistaken for Americans were advised to stay in their hotels. I wondered whether, at short notice, I could get someone to run me up an I-am-not-an-American T-shirt – and then decided it wasn't worth it because I wasn't sure all the NPA could read. Besides, I was assured, there were plenty of other death squads around who just didn't like Westerners full stop; so there really wasn't a lot of point.

I found out quite a lot during the week I was stuck in Manila before the government finally won. I found out that I am not one of nature's war correspondents. I found out that war is a spectator sport. I found out what it feels like to watch from the roof of a hotel with dozens of cheering spectators as an F-5 jet blows a propeller-driven plane out of the sky and into a petrol dump which then burns for two days. (Would you believe that the plane shot down was a Second World War Japanese Zero, of which the Philippine Air Force still has several operational?) I found out that hotel rooms are very boring and that, after a certain amount of vodka, boredom overcomes natural cowardice and you go outside anyway.

And I found out what it's like to spend a lot of time walking around the streets of a city in which many of the people live (in old boxes) lives which compare very unfavourably with the life of the average racehorse. Very unfavourably, in fact, with the life of the average British cat.

I'm afraid I haven't written about the best race meeting I ever went to, although the 1989 Japan Cup was pretty good. (One of the editors of this book had already nicked the best – the 1990 Breeders' Cup – by the time he invited me to do a chapter.) Fragmented memories they may be, but I've written about the trip to the races I'm least likely to forget.

Paul Haigh is chief columnist of the Racing Post, *and author of* The Racehorse Trainer *and* How We Won the Race.

Ian Wooldridge
A ROYALIST REFLECTS

On 23 April 1985, the Princess Royal rode her first race on the Flat at Epsom. She finished fourth on Against The Grain. Recently she wrote about the experience in her book, Riding Through My Life. *Here Against The Grain recalls his own thoughts about that momentous day and takes the opportunity to opine about a few other equestrian matters.*

by AGAINST THE GRAIN

Naturally, since I figure prominently in the book, the publishers sent me an advance copy of *Riding Through My Life*. I took it immediately to my stable – no hardship since I am rather shunned in the yard because of my royal connections – and read it at a sitting. It is extremely good and it was reassuring to see that the Princess's empathy with horses is in direct inverse ratio to her detestation of press photographers. She wrote every word herself, of course.

I confess that, after looking in the index, I took a sneak preview of pages 196 to 201, which are almost all about me. Immediately I was gratified by HRH's observation that Against The Grain's manners 'were a lot better than those of the other horses I had been riding'.

Well, they have to be, don't they, if you are rubbing flanks with royalty? I hate snobbishness but I am greatly concerned about maintaining standards and every day I see them falling all around me. You should just live in one of these yards for a day or two – all that dreadful coughing immediately after breakfast and then, from time to time, those obscene rituals they put us through at breeding time.

But I digress. What particularly interested me about the Princess Royal's account of our race at Epsom was her frank admission that she felt, and I quote, '99 per cent out of control'. That rather alarmed me, I can tell you, the implication being that I, Against The Grain, was 99 per cent *in* control of the destiny of one of the premier royals. And, of course, when you come to think about it, I probably was. I shall have to explain that to my colleagues some morning during work. We've got one chap here who's carried Lester half a dozen times and he definitely needs putting in his place.

Anyway, if the Princess Royal reckoned she was 99 per cent out of control when riding, she was certainly 100 per cent *under* control just before we started. It all happened when suddenly the bars divested themselves of all these oiks in jeans and duffel coats who came rushing on to the course. I distinctly heard one say: 'Jesus, I thought she was riding in the *four*-thirty.'

Permit me to introduce you to the paparazzi, a word of Italian derivation, I understand, to describe men of shameless intrusive capacity. I had assumed they would have brought in Karsh of Ottawa to picture the two of us, but no, here were all these awful tradesmen rushing about. I managed to get one on a knee-cap – nothing trivial I hope – but HRH really rose to the occasion. 'You ever ridden an 'orse?' she demanded of the frightful man from the *Sun*. 'Well then, naff off.'

The expression puzzled me for a moment but then, putting two and two together, I could only assume it was a regal euphemism for a word of similar length in constant usage among the stable lads, particularly on cold mornings. Nor was that the end of it. 'Look 'ere,' she said to another of these rascals, 'if you stick that bloody thing near my 'orse's face again, I'll whack you.' I cannot begin to tell you how my heart went out to her.

I have always had a huge admiration for the upper classes. But, sadly, racing has changed, you know. You should just see some of the types who now classify themselves as 'owners'. Occasionally they come down to visit us in training. They all drive the latest-registration Range Rovers. They wave copies of *Horse and Hound* and shooting sticks, bought the previous day in Harrods. The men wear caps and military warms. The women wear scent and high heels and look as though they think they're going to Henley. And all the time I hear them bleating to the boss about the cost of keeping us in training in accents which, to put it mildly, imply an unorthodox education, if any. What's more, plenty of them don't own more than one-sixteenth of any of us. They only really get into it for a metal owner's badge, a car park pass and the thrill-of-a-lifetime's chance of meeting John Oaksey or being interviewed by Brough Scott.

You can tell the class ones a mile off. The men look as though they've just been through a hedge backwards and they're mostly with someone else's wife. A randy lot, if I'm not mistaken. That, of course, is an area which is a bit of a sore point with some of us down here where we mostly live a pretty dreary monastic existence. Some of us, indeed, will never know The Ultimate Experience, and in depressed moments I even question Britain's reputation as an animal-adoring nation. I mean, they don't go around castrating Prime Ministers or pop singers or cricketers, do they? No, it's only certain members of my fraternity and I have to tell you, in all honesty, that it is deeply resented. Obviously if we were all recidivist rapists like certain members of the human race we'd understand it, but what do we ever do to deserve that treatment?

No, it's not all hay and carrots, I'll have you know. Look at poor old Shergar. Wins everything, minds his own business and gets his head blown off. I met him a couple of times. Absolute gent. So the IRA knock him off and to this day his killers go unapprehended. No point capturing them really, is there? They'd be let out again as soon as some smart lawyer suggests the police cooked up the evidence. You humans amaze us sometimes. We have a thing called horse sense and what occurs to us is if these people didn't kill Shergar and lots of lovely ordinary people in pubs all over the country, then who did? We have an altogether harsher discipline in the racing game.

I do keep getting myself sidetracked. But that's understandable because we get a lot of time for contemplation and not too much to read: *Sporting Life* and *Racing Post*, of course, and an occasional *Telegraph* and *Harpers & Queen*. I loved *Harpers*, because I thought Jennifer's Diary represented the true British way of life. Now, of course, she's retired and I don't quite know where to turn. It certainly won't be to that *Playboy* magazine. I found a copy once which some stable boys must have inadvertently left in my box. If that's what women owners look like undressed, thank God they come down here with their clothes on.

The Minister of Sport came once, shouting things like 'Ho, ho, so this is the famous Against The Grain.' He struck me as knowing as much about racing as I do about Lloyd's broking. Naturally the boss told him about my royal connection. The Minister was instantly alert: 'Do you really mean,' he said, 'that this is the one the Queen rides at Trooping the Colour?' There's one born every minute. He kept patronizingly patting me on the nose, so obviously I bit him. And do you know something? Because there were photographers present he *kept on smiling*.

Well, that's about it really. We came fourth that day at Epsom, the Princess Royal and I. She was really gracious afterwards and didn't walk away immediately as though I didn't exist. I greatly appreciated her consideration and that night, back in my box, I hummed a verse or two of the National Anthem.

Ian Wooldridge has worked for the Daily Mail *since 1961. Formerly their cricket writer, he is now chief sports writer and columnist. Although ignorant about racing, he is very enthusiastic.*

The old, the bold and the barmy

Clement Freud
FIRST LEARN THE LANGUAGE

The French use the word 'ancien' not as we do to denote antiquity but to mean 'used to be'. At a recent dinner in France my host, who had done his homework with un-gallic thoroughness, introduced me as 'un ancien jockey', indicating that I have had the odd ride in public (*jockey* – like *outsider* and *walkover*, also *deadheat* – is an international word, though pronounced differently in different countries). Well, having been a jockey is one of the things for which I rather like to be remembered. It happened in my early middle-age, which is elderly for a man setting out on a career in the saddle, and was the result of a new racehorse-owner's inability to understand trainer-speak.

It was the late 1960s, Harold Wilson reigned at Number 10, and the budget for that year disallowed as an acceptable business expense all entertainment, even breakfasts, luncheon, tea and dinner bills, except where the object of hospitality was an overseas buyer. At the Newmarket sales in October I bought an Ananmestes yearling and named him Overseas Buyer. It was my intention to claim his expenses against tax: training bills would be entered as 'accommodating overseas buyer', racecourse visits as 'monitoring overseas buyer', bets as 'testing overseas buyer's market'.

I gave him to Toby Balding and some weeks after he was first saddled phoned my young trainer to ask how things were going.

Come and see him work, he said; we'll put you up.

I brought my pyjamas.

He meant ride out.

I didn't like to say that I had not ridden for thirty years, and then not seriously, unless you count the leading-rein class at the Blythburgh Gymkhana; also one journalistic day's hunting with the Quorn for the *Sunday Telegraph*, followed by five days in bed to get over it.

I was given a leg up on a three-mile hurdler due to run for his life in a seller at Newton Abbot later that week, and did what the stable lads in front of and behind and beside me did. An hour later, at breakfast, before my two-year-old was due to go out with the second lot, I asked Toby how he thought I had ridden.

Better than some bloody amateurs who try to go faster than the horse, said he. I was chuffed.

I worked for the original, pre-page-three *Sun* as a sports writer at the time. Be provocative, said the sports editor, the way sports editors do. I wrote a piece about bloody amateur jockeys going faster than their horses, and invariably putting up overweight, which could not appear in the racing papers because it is libellous to write that bets on Moonstruck are not a good idea as the owner Mr J. Johnson (7) is not only useless and unable to claim his allowance but is likely to weigh out 12lb heavy. Johnson would only have to have one leg amputated to take you to court.

Good piece, said my sports editor. Why don't you have a go?

I explained that God had not built me to race-ride, that I had not weighed under 13st 5lb since I left the army after the war, twenty years earlier.

The sports editor was unimpressed. The most unlikely people ride, he said, and I thought about it for a while, discussed becoming a latter-day Gordon Richards with Toby Balding, who was by then a friend as well as my trainer, and embarked on the campaign of losing two stone in ten weeks, in the course of which I would also achieve uncommon fitness, a shape that needed a new wardrobe and gave me near-terminal halitosis.

Reluctant to manifest my prowess in the saddle before my own countrymen, I wrote to the Irish Jockey Club for an amateur's licence, sending with my application a coolish assessment of my skills on horseback signed by G. B. Balding. The Stewards of the Irish Jockey Club, in their wisdom, decided to inspect me in person, so I flew to Dublin and presented myself at their offices in Merrion Square wearing a suit with a 32-inch waist, in from 38 inches.

They looked at me with mild curiosity and the senior man asked how long I had been riding, casually, as one horsey man to another.

I can tell you that exactly, I said. It is now 4 September. I started on 29 July.

There was an intake of breaths and a splutter.

The Senior Steward looked me up and down incredulously and said: 'Have you done any speed work?'

I explained that it had been nearly all speed work; to date I had found it hard to stop horses from doing speed work . . . which was surely what racing was about. Before them, I intimated, stood a man who would never be called before the men with hats for pulling a horse.

I got my licence ('What harm can he do?' said one of the Stewards) and after a warning against importuning people for mounts, I returned to England and a lesson from Mr James Lindley, a stylist whom I much admired. He watched me on the Weyhill gallops and opined that if I looked less like a . . . .ing policeman I might well manage to look more like a jockey. As a consequence I raised my irons and learnt to bend my spine; and in God's good time one of Toby's owners, a brave Irishman called Joe Hehir who was a power in the used tyre trade in Kilkenny and a fierce consumer of proof spirit, offered me a mount in a bumper at Naas, set to carry 12st 7lb. I could make that. There was a 7lb allowance for having ridden less than a certain number of winners. I found that difficult.

I also found it difficult to get into the jockeys' changing room. A man stopped me, said This is the jockeys' changing room.

I said I know that.

He said Well you can't go in, I mean I know who you are, but I can't let you through.

I said I am a jockey.

He said Never.

He probably had a point . . . though I was in the lead first time round and realized, which I had not thought about in all the years in which I had gone racing, that you don't have to look round to see where the rest of the field is as you can hear the commentary.

Over the next eighteen months I rode when I could. Had a tricky time at Leicester when my mount squeezed me against the side of the stall and I emerged with my left foot along its spine; it took me a furlong to get back into position and I read in the following day's *Sporting Life* that I had 'dwelt at the start'. At Bath, before another race for which I had fasted and used diuretics to make the weight, my trainer looked at me in the parade ring and gave me a spoonful of salt in a glass of water to stop me from seizing up. I vomited for a mile and a half and tried to clean the saddle with my whip . . .

81

But my finest hour came in a Match race against Hugh Fraser at Haydock. I had challenged him. We both took it v. seriously, both broke ribs and sustained bruises about the body getting fit, both backed ourselves extravagantly with the on-course book-makers – one of whom offered 5–1 on either rider to finish alone, which gave me some confidence. I had flown over the course and ridden it and walked it on the morning of the race. I was on Winter Fair, whom I had bought out of Ian Balding's yard where he was galloping companion to Mill Reef, and just a little of that brilliance rubbed off. Sir Hugh was riding one of his horses set to carry a stone less than mine and the tapes went up and because we were both pretty average jockeys and my horse was better than his, I won. Had not realized that racing was as simple as that.

I considered riding another nineteen winners to reduce my allowance but didn't think I could shed any more weight. Not long after that I hung up my 12oz saddle and my breath improved.

Clement Freud is a cook/journalist/politician and has been a lover of racing since backing the Ascot Gold Cup winner in 1934. He lives in London and Suffolk; holidays in Portugal where he has to buy lottery tickets.

John Oaksey
THE BOGMAN AND THE BARRISTER

'At least you will be riding the fittest horse.' Surveying Proud Tarquin's rivals before the 1974 Whitbread Gold Cup, Roddy Armytage did not sound particularly confident. But he was, almost certainly, dead right.

Of course, it is not much good being fit if you are also exhausted and Proud Tarquin might easily have been both. In the seven days before the Whitbread he had travelled about a thousand miles by road and run a hard, losing race (well, as hard as I could give him) against Red Rum over the four miles of the Scottish Grand National. Now, compelled by his rider's middle-age spread to put up 8lb overweight, he was taking on the previous year's Gold Cup winner The Dikler and fourteen others round two rock-hard circuits of Sandown Park.

A month past my 45th birthday I was lucky to be riding in such a race at all, luckier still to be riding for Roddy Armytage and luckiest of all to be wearing the orange and white colours of Sir John Thomson — a special light silk version bought to help my battle with the scales!

Ten years earlier my first ride for Roddy, on an inappropriately named horse called Pioneer Spirit, had ended in ignominious disaster. Landing nearly a fence clear over the second last at Cheltenham I somehow decided that I had taken the wrong course —and pulled poor Pioneer Spirit up. Heedless of my warning cries, the only other survivor Bill Tellwright swept past with a look of mingled pity and contempt ... The crowd booed, the Stewards fined me £25 — and Roddy Armytage might easily never have spoken to me again. Instead, he and Sue became two of my best and firmest friends — and among the many splendid rides they gave me were various sons of Sir John Thomson's immortal steeplechasing matriarch Leney Princess.

One of them, Tuscan Prince, is grazing outside the window as I write – winner of thirteen 'chases, hero of numerous Team Events, kindly point-to-point schoolmaster to my daughter Sara and, touch wood, going strong at 27. By Black Tarquin and almost black himself, 'Tuscy' is a year younger than but otherwise virtually the identical twin of Proud Tarquin, who himself died some years ago after a happy retirement spent hunting with Colin Nash and the Old Berks. Their most distinguished brother, Fort Leney, won a Cheltenham Gold Cup and, between them, Leney Princess's sons and grandsons have won a grand total of eighty-five steeplechases. They all started their racing careers with the late Tom Dreaper and their devoted owner-breeder Sir John Thomson is now happily married to the great Irish trainer's widow Betty.

Almost all Leney Princess's sons have been 'characters' in one way or another. Prince Tino, who won as a fifteen-year-old, used to keep you standing for up to half an hour outside his box. The worse the weather the longer he stood there – before suddenly plunging in to confront the resident ghost of his imagination. When first retired, Proud Tarquin (who stood nearly seventeen hands) jumped out of his loose-box *through the top door* – without bothering to open, or even break, the bottom one. He did cut his knees on the concrete yard outside but was otherwise none the worse. He became a superb hunter and the Old Berks hounds were often actually hunted from his back.

Second as an eight-year-old in the Irish Grand National, 'Tarkie' (they all had abbreviated and somewhat unimaginative nicknames!) gave me a wonderful ride in Red Rum's – or, more properly, Crisp's – record-breaking 1973 epic at Aintree. But, though seventh that day – finishing, Sir John always swears, inside the previous record time – he was not qualified for the Aintree Grand National of 1974. Hence our presence at Ayr and Sandown.

By that time we had discovered that blinkers were the key to Tarkie's habitually lethargic attitude. The first time they were applied he trotted up at Taunton and from then on, instead of exhausting hard labour, riding him became, at least for the first three-quarters of his races, a delight. But the family 'kink' was still there lying in wait. I shall never, for instance, forget a disgraceful day at Lingfield when, landing over the last with a race at his mercy, Tarkie hung so violently left that another horse was able to get up and pip us on the line. There is no running rail from the last at Lingfield and, shamefully unable to switch my whip in time, I was carried, willy-nilly, at 45 degrees across the track!

There was no repetition of that at Ayr – simply the frustration of being left standing on the flat by Red Rum. He was, of course, completing an historic double in that year's English and Scottish Grand Nationals and was, I suspect, as good that day as at any time in his unique career. That Scottish National was, in fact, a contest of rare all-round distinction – with Proud Tarquin very nearly caught and deprived of second place by a horse called Kildagin. 'Who's he?' you may well ask. I will tell you.

In August 1991 I was invited to visit the Belgian equivalent of our Grand National – the Grand Steeplechase de Flandres run at Warregem. This is an amazing contest round a razor-sharp track over obstacles which include an Irish bank, a white post-and-rails with water behind it, a 'double' and several other Auteuil-type barriers, dauntingly unfamiliar to the average British 'chaser. There is only the one day's racing at Warregem each year; the whole town stops work and a jolly, noisy crowd of more than 30,000 packs the stands. It is a notable sporting occasion with its own unforgettable holiday atmosphere; and not once but twice in the 1970s Kildagin was its hero. Trained by David Nicholson and ridden by John Suthern, he mastered the problems of Warregem well enough to beat the locals, and in the small but enthusiastic world of Belgian steeplechasing Kildagin is an honoured name. But he was only third best at Ayr and Proud Tarquin, who gave him a stone, arrived back at East Ilsley showing no sign whatever of his exertions. He was in such high spirits, in fact, that, after much thought and discussion, Roddy persuaded a somewhat reluctant Sir John to run again just seven days later.

Whitbread Gold Cup day at Sandown has always been my favourite occasion of the whole racing year – the best of both Flat and jumping on the best course of them all. The 1974 Classic Trial produced a significant if somewhat misleading result when the subsequent St Leger winner Bustino beat his subsequent Derby conqueror Snow Knight. But by that time Classic prospects were the last thing on my mind. Hard ground is an all-too-common feature of the Whitbread and Proud Tarquin would certainly have preferred it a bit softer. As a result, for the first two and a half miles, with Cuckolder and Credo's Daughter setting a furious gallop, he was, quite literally, going as fast as he could lay legs to the ground.

Riding round Sandown in such a contest can be a dream or a nightmare – quite often both. The close fences down the Railway straight put such a high premium on quick, clean, accurate jumping that the slightest check or hesitation is apt to leave you struggling. Ground lost in the air just cannot be won back on the flat – not without spending energy which, with three miles and five furlongs to go, you can ill afford. Each fence is a little crisis, but in 1974 I do not remember Proud Tarquin, God bless him, making even the semblance of a mistake. Down the back for the last time, he jumped up to pass Credo's Daughter and, since finishing speed has never been his strongest weapon, there seemed no point in waiting any longer. As we led round the final bend an encouraging medley of slaps and shouts suggested that by no means all our pursuers were finding chasing us a picnic. But then, going to the second last, a large, white, all too easily recognizable face loomed up beside my knee. Much as I like and admire Ron Barry, he and The Dikler were, at that moment, the least welcome sight you could possibly imagine.

Earlier, remembering Lingfield and hoping that forewarned might be forearmed, I had laboriously manoeuvred the whip through to my left hand. So I was uncharacteristically well prepared when, landing over the last half a length in front, Proud Tarquin played his same old favourite trick. But this time, as he ducked left-handed towards The Dikler, I gave him a sharp clout on the left side of his head and, from there to the line no railway ever ran straighter.

The damage, alas, was done. No contact, let alone 'bump', occurred but if The Dikler had spent half his life at RADA he could scarcely have played the role of 'injured party' with more gusto. Cowering away, he did, briefly but unquestionably, break stride and, at the line, the camera showed Proud Tarquin only a bare head in front.

'Well done – but you came over a bit' was Ron Barry's ominous comment as we pulled up, and the announcement 'Stewards' Enquiry' followed hard on the Judge's verdict.

The Dikler's trainer Fulke Walwyn, winner of six Whitbreads (one of them my own on Taxidermist in 1958) did not compile that unique record by leaving much to chance. So an objection 'pour encourager' was quickly lodged.

'What chance have you got – a poor old bogman against a barrister?', Monty Court asked Ron Barry as we stood waiting for the Stewards' verdict. But Monty, shrewd old hack that he is, got this one wrong three ways. I was never qualified as a barrister, I would certainly not call Ron, then the reigning champion and now an Inspector of Courses, 'a poor old bogman' – and the Stewards disqualified Proud Tarquin! As so often in such cases, the head-on film made the whole thing look much worse than it felt at the time either to me or to Ron – whose evidence was scrupulously fair. So the Stewards (two of whom were young enough to be my sons and had minimal experience of steeplechasing) cannot really be blamed for feeling that the interference *might* have made a head's worth of difference.

Funnily enough the 1974 Whitbread is not, for me, an unhappy memory – except on behalf of Sir John Thomson, Roddy Armytage and Proud Tarquin's lad. Unlike most of my other race-riding disasters I never felt that I did much wrong at Sandown. To tell the truth, non-swanks, I have always been rather proud of staying a head in front of Ron Barry after riding 200 yards of a finish with the whip in my left hand. As for Proud Tarquin, no one ever told him he was disqualified . . .

John Oaksey rode as an amateur for 20 years and is still writing about racing and occasionally talking about it on television. He was once a quite close second in the Grand National and is the only person known to have pulled up when a fence in front because he thought he had gone the wrong way at Cheltenham.

Brough Scott
WHO'S A PARTY POOPER NOW?

It wasn't me that was crooked. A winner over jumps, the first time, the best time; but for me a memory that should not be.

Chepstow, 26 October 1963. No motorway yet across the Severn so it would have been the long golden autumn journey beside the river from Gloucester through villages like Minsterworth and Westbury. Or if you came further west, you wound down the Wye past Wordsworth's ruined inspiration of Tintern Abbey.

Recollections blur together down the years and it was probably before another Chepstow ride that we were lucky to escape the police pen. Stopped the car at a top-of-the-hill sweetshop in Lydney, didn't apply the hand-brake and so returned to find no motor. Terrible slow downward swivel of the head located car at the bottom of the hill sprawled across the war memorial!

No confusion in the memory of the race itself. The Monmouth Handicap Hurdle, thirteen runners over two miles, the favourite Cotswold ridden by local trainer–rider Colin Davies, my horse the beloved black oil painting that was Arcticeelagh. He was eight years old now and still an entire; he looked after himself. In an earlier life he had been a McGrath Classic hope in Ireland. Compared to the usual hairy-heeled jumper he was an aesthete. He had a slightly parrot mouth and his near fore dished a little at the canter. But his eye burned with intelligence and his coat shone like silk. This was elegance on the hoof.

The trouble was that Arcticeelagh delighted in taking things carefully, at a pace to suit himself. Dad had bought him that spring for something like 800 guineas. The idea was that at this stage he might 'go better for a boy'. Well, he might. If he wanted to. In a race he had two quite distinct gaits. One was a delicate, fastidious old gentleman's gallop. He would consent to take part in the contest but very much on his own terms, no hassle, ease off the heroics. But then there was the other gear, the Classic shift. The one that could win anything. If ever you could engage it.

He had first run for us at Cheltenham that April. It was my second ride under Rules; the first had been at Woore a fortnight earlier on a willing but untalented mare called Tamhill. It was a 28-runner novice hurdle. We beat two. Next stop Prestbury Park was like playing your second game at Wembley. Arcticeelagh, at least, had been there before. He had actually run in the Champion Hurdle as a five-year-old. But he was eight now. This was quite a competitive handicap and right from the start the old boy was in no mood to take chances.

Very soon we were out among the tail-enders. Arcticeelagh's neck curled back carefully as he picked his way along the outside, the tilted ears threatening an all-out strike if I pressed my amateurish urgings too hard. All the way down the back straight we trundled along like this. And on up to the crown of the hill with me getting ever more desperate to avoid disgrace, Arcticeelagh apparently heedless of all the effort and dreams that had been invested by the flapping 20-year-old in the saddle above. Then, at the very top of the slope, he took pity, remembered his calling, abandoned veteran status, and was a racehorse again.

From tittupping old gentleman he was suddenly transformed into a thoroughbred stretched long and greyhound-low in the gallop. I was at the ultra-novice stage when you don't even feel the mud on your goggles. I had never been, have never been, as fast in my life. The air whistled through the mane, the third last hurdle was taken with the bound of a coursing cheetah. Down the hill we tore and horses which had seemed distant specks on the horizon were reeled back into focus. He finished so fast we were only beaten three lengths. Third. To Fred Winter at Cheltenham. Incredible.

But the gear change was at Articeelagh's choosing and sometimes he didn't engage it at all. He gave another late burst to be third at Uttoxeter, then he so completely pulled my leg at Salisbury and Epsom that one embarrassingly awful morning we put blinkers on him and Frenchie Nicholson sang the hunting crop across those black satin hindquarters. Arcticeelagh was furious and horrified. But it did the trick. Next time out we went to Lingfield. Once the blinkers were on, Arcticeelagh dragged old Ted round the paddock as if the electrodes had been fitted. He was still lit up at the start. We made all the running and beat the 'good thing' of Hern's by a neck. My father had backed us at 33–1. They could hear his shouting as far away as Southampton Water.

Lightning has trouble with the second strike. But, filtered back through hindsight, the road to Chepstow had an inevitability about it. After a rest, we ran Arcticeelagh over hurdles at Wincanton and left off the blinkers to invite co-operation rather than compulsion. He declined. Some honour in fourth place to Ian Balding but Arcticeelagh couldn't fool us that he was trying. So 'blinds' on again at Chepstow. No saddling-ring panic this time but his teeth were grinding darkly as he was led in for the leg-up. Frenchie took my arm in that lovely stern-uncle but greatest-supporter way of his. 'You know what to do. Keep hold of him. Kid him. Make him feel good.' Oh, the waking dream of it all!

I was very inexperienced but Arcticeelagh wasn't. This was his day, you could almost sense it. He was feeling good. He was a class apart. I didn't know enough to mess it up. This time there was no hectic all-the-way desperation. In our own way we stalked the field, the rookie and the old rogue. It didn't seem that difficult. On the long downhill run away from the river we began to pick off the others. Up the straight he didn't have the supercharge of Cheltenham but we had the leaders in our sights. From the second last the ground rolls you beautifully into the final flight. Two horses to beat but we had them covered. Nimble quick at the last; now the shouting began. Great waves of it down from the stands and from the rows of spectators above us on the Chepstow slope. But there was another infinitely closer yell going up. It was my voice screaming into Arcticeelagh's half-cocked ears to get us home.

The old boy obliged. Not by much, and a bit grudgingly for sure. But all the way up that run-in he felt as if we would get the best of things. Fifty yards out we had inched ahead. A narrow advantage and Arcticeelagh on the point of crying enough. But the post rushed up and past with us still just in charge. We had done it. We had planned it and had delivered. No Derby or National rider supped a moment more sweet. Nothing could take away the taste.

Well, not quite. Afterwards it was all an excited whirl of jubilation. The steep walk back up to the winners' circle. The sense of unreality turning to hold-your-breath concern as we lugged the saddle over to the scales for the weigh-in. The glowing pride of parents, the cat-with-the-cream conceit of favoured son. Yes, 'that was the plan'.

Later, no doubt, there were bolder celebrations, probably starting with a drink or three at The Highwayman on that old Roman road from Birdlip to Cirencester. The victor's tale would be extending deep into self-glorification. No one would have had the wish nor the wit to spoil the party by reading the small print of the Stewards' report. But it's true. I may remember it as the finest, most forceful ride since Dick Turpin set poor old Black Bess off towards the Knavesmire but the facts must have been rather different. Amidst the back-slapping we didn't notice the hustle in the Stewards' room. Things had looked so bad that the second jock was warned off for not trying.

Maybe, but the memory still glows, happily distorted with yours truly as hero. Who'll be a party-pooper now?

Brough Scott, who rode 100 winners as an amateur and professional jockey, is editorial director of the Racing Post *and senior presenter on Channel Four Racing. He was racing correspondent of* The Sunday Times *before joining the* Independent on Sunday *in 1989, and is the author of* The World of Flat Racing, On and Off the Rails *and* Front Runners.

Peter Scudamore
EXCESSIVE USE OF THE ELBOW

Some of the most eventful days' racing I have had have been overseas. I have ridden in Europe, Scandinavia, America, Australia and New Zealand, either as a team member of the British Jump Jockeys or as an individual.

Norway is among the smaller racing nations that I have visited, but none the less fun and friendly for it. Øvrevoll is its only racecourse; situated just outside the capital, Oslo, among the surrounding mountains, hills and trees, it is a most picturesque track.

There is very little jump racing in Norway – only one or two races on a card. The hurdle races take place on the Flat track, which is left-handed and about 2,000 metres round. The hurdles are not to my liking. They are about 1 metre high, made of wood with birch woven through them. They look very similar to a small thin portable fence, and here lies the problem; to keep them upright they have stabilizers in front of them which are not driven into the ground, so if a horse in front of you hits one hard by the time you arrive to jump the hurdle it can be revolving in the air!

The steeplechase course is a figure of eight, like Fontwell, on the inside of the Flat race track, and the fences are of the continental type where horses have to jump through the fence, rather than over it as with the British and Irish steeplechase fence. Although these fences are big on a very sharp track, I prefer to ride over them rather than their hurdles.

One of the highlights of the Norwegian racing year – most of the racing takes place through the summer months – is the Norwegian Grand National which happens in the autumn as racing is only just getting going in England. The obvious advantage to any National Hunt jockey going to ride over there is the fact that racing takes place on a Sunday, so you do not have to miss any racing in England.

One trip I remember particularly well. I had flown over to Oslo from Heathrow with a number of other jockeys. The fun began in the first race of the day, a hurdle race, when one of the Norwegian jockeys, who had been stood down by the Stewards at a previous meeting for hitting his horse, decided to get his own back on the Stewards for his punishment.

He started off by pretending to be drunk. He rode very short anyway, but as he was leaving the paddock he kept flopping down either side of his horse, and while cantering to the start he stood on the rump of the horse until he arrived at the practice hurdle – which you jump on the way to the start in most countries – when he pulled up, put his feet in the irons and jumped the hurdle normally before proceeding to the start. In the race, instead of adopting a jockey's position between the hurdles he stood bolt upright looking from side to side to point out to all in the race what he was doing! His horse was the favourite, and came to the last hurdle upsides in front, but instead of riding for the line, he took his stick and threw it at one of the Stewards' Boxes by the side of the course; he then proceeded to hit his horse down the shoulder with his elbow. By this time he had been overtaken by another horse, and was beaten, much to the disapproval of the crowd and the trainer of the horse. The Stewards were not too amused either, and I never saw him ride again!

The National was a relatively tame event after this, and I got round in third place. One of the other English riders whom I had given a lift to the airport, because we both had to go to Southwell the next day, was John Suthern. I had very kindly got John a spare ride in this race, as I was already booked, but it only had one eye – and I forgot to mention this to John until we arrived in Norway. The one eye was not enough for the horse to negotiate the fences safely, so John had a fall – a fairly easy one.

The Norwegians are very hospitable people, and organized a wonderful party for us all in a night club in Oslo, from which we crawled away in the early hours of the morning – John had asked me to stay close by him to make sure that nobody stood on his hands as he crawled back to the hotel! The next morning we had to leave very early to catch the first plane to London, all of us by this time feeling a lot worse from the previous night's exploits. John was complaining about his back, which he said had caught a chill, and was aching, and he could only relieve the pain by sitting hunched up in his chair. He flew like this to Heathrow, the journey taking longer than anticipated as we seemed to circle endlessly above London waiting to land.

We were late landing; this meant a mad dash to Southwell, which is just north of Nottingham with the last part of the journey being particularly twisty and slow. John was crouched in his huddled position in the front of my car, in full flow of complaint at me for having got him the ride in Norway, and now it looked as though he was going to miss his fancied ride in the first at Southwell because we were so late. I was definitely feeling twinges of guilt and drove as fast as I could. We made it to the track twenty minutes before the race; dashing to the weighing room we saw another jockey in John's horse's colours just about to weigh out, so I grabbed the colours off the substitute jockey before he could do so, while John hurriedly changed and then weighed out. We now had about five minutes before the race, so John and I were telling the other jockeys about our exploits in Norway, and how all's well that ends well, and how pleased we were to have arrived at Southwell on time. John went out to ride; I went to get changed for my race later on that afternoon, before watching John's race on the closed circuit television. I was delighted to see John come to the last in front . . . before he fell!

Peter Scudamore has been champion National Hunt Jockey for the last six seasons, and shared the title in 1981/82 with John Francome. He has ridden more winners than any other jump jockey in history, and his 1988/89 total of 221 victories is a record for a single season.

Dick Francis
FINNURE

My two most satisfactory and satisfying days at the races were both to do with one horse – Lord Bicester's Finnure. He may be mostly forgotten now, but to me he was the perfect horse, the absolute star. By Cacador, Finnure was bred to be a very good racehorse for both the Flat and steeplechasing, and indeed, before becoming the property of that most dedicated of jumping owners, Lord Bicester, he had already shown his prowess on the Flat by winning the Irish Cesarewitch.

Finnure was a fine, big, upstanding golden chestnut. Beautifully proportioned, full of quality, he had a most intelligent head, with an eye packed full of interest. He had a fine shoulder in front of the saddle, which, incidentally, sat in a perfect position and gave the rider the impression he couldn't possibly fall off. Unlike Roimond, another of the same owner's great well-muscled steeplechasing stars of yesteryear, he wasn't at all cumbersome, but when one sat on Finnure one seemed to be looking down on all those around. His stride was long and flowing; he took just a nice hold of the bit and I could tell a long way before he got to a fence in just which stride he would take off to jump, adjusting my rhythm accordingly to match his. Crudwell, winner of over fifty races, was the only other mount I rode who had equal awareness and power of transmitting his intentions to his rider.

My first ride on Finnure, at the now defunct Birmingham racecourse, was a winning one, and of the total of seven races in which I rode him before the 1951 Grand National, we won every one.

Our first big moment together was in 1949 in the King George VI Steeplechase, the showpiece of Kempton Park's Christmas Meeting.

Fortunately, both for the horse and for me, a severe frost on the morning of 26 December had necessitated the big Boxing Day card being postponed for twenty-four hours. I had time to recover from Christmas turkey and Finnure, who had travelled to Kempton and back on the 26th, had not been subjected to trainer George Beeby's usual policy of giving his horses a severe work-out the day before they were to run. Consequently, Finnure lined up at Kempton on the 27th a somewhat fresh horse.

In the same big race twelve months earlier I had been runner-up on Lord Bicester's Roimond to the renowned Irish challenger, Cottage Rake, and it was my greatest desire to get my revenge in 1949 on Vincent O'Brien's star, then unbeaten on British soil. Coming second to him had made me all too painfully aware of the winning tactics usually adopted by Cottage Rake's great Irish jockey, Aubrey Brabazon, and consequently I gave a lot of thought to the tactics I planned to adopt. These crystallized in essence as keeping closely within touch of Cottage Rake and not letting him get away unexpectedly into an accelerating lead.

Luckily, Finnure being such an easy horse to manoeuvre, this proved possible. Within the field of only half a dozen or so runners I managed to stay on Cottage Rake's heels all the way, coming round the last bend into the straight a scant length behind him, with another two horses in front. In those days Kempton Park had only two fences after rounding the final bend, and Brabazon made his challenge at about the same place as he had against Roimond the year before, just as the leaders were approaching the second-to-last fence. Finnure and I jumped this particular fence about a length behind Cottage Rake, and, moments later, as we were approaching the last fence of all, I realized my mount was meeting it absolutely in his stride. I asked him for a major effort and this he gave, and with the momentum with which we were travelling, we passed Cottage Rake in mid-air and landed full of running about three-quarters of a length to the good. From that point on the battle really commenced, the two horses giving their all and galloping away from the opposition. Finnure and I came out on top and finished a neck in front of Cottage Rake at the post.

I got indescribable satisfaction from this result; not only did it enable Finnure (my most favourite horse) to become the first to lower Cottage Rake's colours on British soil, it also proved that I

Walter Swinburn steers Shergar to his record-breaking win in the 1981 Derby . . .

... and five years later the same connections are celebrating again as Shahrastani holds off Dancing Brave and Greville Starkey to unleash controversy

'Monkey' – Waggoners Walk – out on his own at the last fence in the 1981 Kim Muir Chase at Cheltenham

The great Secretariat at Claiborne Farm near Paris, Kentucky

Desert Orchid and Simon Sherwood return to unsaddle after their 1989 Cheltenham Gold Cup triumph. A few lengths behind, a figure in deerstalker and dark glasses joins in the applause

The Princess Royal hardly looks '99 per cent out of control' as she rides Against The Grain to the start of the Farriers Private Sweepstakes at Epsom in 1985

A whirlwind finish from Lester Piggott gets Royal Academy up to beat Itsallgreektome in the 1990 Breeders' Cup Mile at Belmont Park

The last fence in two unforgettable Grand Nationals. *Above*, Red Rum and Tommy Stack in 1977. *Opposite*, Aldaniti and Bob Champion in 1981

The 1990 Breeders' Cup at Belmont Park. *Above*, Dayjur and Willie Carson hurdle the shadow as Safely Kept keeps going to win. *Below*, The tragic end to an unforgettable race as Go For Wand crashes into the rails, leaving Bayakoa to score a hollow victory

could hold my own in a hard-fought finish with a great jockey like Aubrey Brabazon, who was equally adept at riding tight finishes on the Flat as he was at riding over hurdles and fences. The welcome back we received that day from the large Christmas holiday crowd was terrific; and seeing the smiles of not only Lord Bicester, but my wife and my father as well, as we were being led in, is something I have cherished to this day.

These most pleasurable moments were to be repeated three months later, when Finnure and I lined up for what subsequently proved to be the final running of the once renowned and popular Champion 'Chase at Aintree's Grand National meeting.

In those days the Grand National was always run on the middle day, Friday, of the three-day spring meeting, and the Champion 'Chase on the Saturday. In 1949 I rode Roimond in the Grand National but finished second to Russian Hero. The following day I rode another of Lord Bicester's great horses, Silver Fame, in the Champion 'Chase, taking on Freebooter, the pride of Yorkshire with a string of starry successes to his name. Silver Fame, full of running, came crashing down at the last fence when upsides with Freebooter in the lead. He lay winded for so long that poor Lord Bicester hurried on foot down the course, very distressed, someone having wrongly told him his horse was dead. Silver Fame, Roimond and Finnure were as dear to him as his children.

The following year, 1950, Freebooter won the Grand National on the Friday. I again rode Roimond, but we came a cropper at the fence after Bechers' first time round. On the Saturday, in the Champion, I set off on Finnure in somewhat low spirits and embarked on a duel against Coloured Schoolboy, another first-class steeplechaser. I can't now explain the low spirits, as there I was on my favourite horse on my favourite course in a field of only four or five runners, but I started that last Champion 'Chase in the grip of glooms.

The start of the Champion 'Chase was over where the Melling Road crosses the Anchor Bridge, about six furlongs from the winning post. It was quite a gallop to the first fence (this being the thirteenth and twenty-ninth of the Grand National course) and consequently fresh Champion 'Chase runners were going at quite a speed by the time they reached it. However, Finnure met this first fence absolutely in his stride – as was his wont! – and jumped it superbly. Immediately alongside us was Coloured Schoolboy, ridden by Arthur Thompson, and from this point onwards Arthur and I never saw another horse. We were right out on our own, both horses jumping equally well, neither giving or taking an inch throughout the whole of the race which proved to be a ding-dong struggle from start to finish; and somewhere along the way my depression lifted like mist.

For the first two miles, that is until we came on to the racecourse proper for the second time, Arthur and I were throwing remarks to each other on how our horses had negotiated the fences we had just jumped. This banter stopped as we began the final six furlongs, but we still jumped the last two fences in perfect unison and harmony. From the last fence battle really started, both our mounts giving of their all. My own came out the better in the end by just a neck. Down-in-the-dumps had soared into euphoria! It was a race I shall always remember, and was easily the one I gained most enjoyment from – *my greatest race.*

It was twelve months later, in 1951, that Finnure and I set out with what I thought was my best chance ever of winning the Grand National itself. Unfortunately, though, the Starter let the thirty-plus runners off in the most ragged of starts, some of the horses and their jockeys even facing in the opposite direction. Consequently there was a disorganized high-speed charge of most of the runners to the first fence, with jockeys struggling to get at least a 'sight' of what they were about to jump. Beforehand, trainer George Beeby had reminded me not to go too fast early on, Finnure being a horse who took a fair bit of time to warm up to the task in front of him. So, having made a reasonable get-away, and not being one of those engaged in a mad rush for the first fence, I was very much in the second battalion approaching it.

While we were in mid-air both my mount and I could see below us a whole mass of horses either falling or struggling to their feet, *ten* already having parted company with their riders. Finnure landed absolutely perfectly over the obstacle, but in side-stepping to miss one of those staggering to their feet he slipped up and thus became faller No. 11. The fall unfortunately resulted in his twisting his hock so badly that he was never any good again. A very sorry end to racing for a very good and brave horse.

For me, riding Finnure was one of the greatest delights of my racing career. A long time before we got to any particular fence he would prick his ears in anticipation of jumping. It was an action which always reminded me of Snaffles' famous painting 'The Finest View in Europe', a picture of a foxhunting man's point of view while sitting on his grey horse following the huntsman and his hounds in full cry, about to set off across beautiful hunting country. For me, the best view on any racecourse was ahead through the pricked ears of Finnure.

My old friend ended his days on Newmarket Heath as trainer Bruce Hobbs's hack, given for this purpose by Lord Bicester. For some years his loping stride was seen leading the yearlings and two-year-olds in their initial work on the heath. He loved his schoolmasterly retirement.

Owing to his wife Mary's asthmatic problems, Dick Francis now lives full-time in Florida. 1991 was a tip-top year for Dick; he not only published his thirtieth novel (Comeback), but he was also awarded the honorary degree of Doctor of Humane Letters by Tufts University, Boston, Massachusetts.

Lester Piggott
ANOTHER YELLOW CARD . . .

In the seventies I used to spend part of each winter in the Far East on a working holiday which led to frequent flights between Hong Kong and Singapore.

At that time British Airways' greatest asset as far as many racing people were concerned was Steve Stanford, who represented the airline's Customer Relations Department. Steve, one of the few 'outsiders' to receive a regular invitation to the Jockeys' Annual Dinner, handled bookings for most of us riders. He got us on flights at the last minute, accelerated formalities, sped his clients to the aircraft on departure and met them on arrival. When minutes counted, as they often did, Steve was a saviour. But when I needed him most we were separated by seven thousand miles.

On this particular weekend I'd got a ride in the last at Sha Tin (Hong Kong) on Saturday and one in the first the next afternoon at Bukit Timah (Singapore) where, more importantly, I had a good chance in the Lion City Cup – the premier sprint of the season. I'd won it twice before and there was no way I wanted to miss that.

In those days flights between Hong Kong and Singapore were seldom direct, especially at weekends. There should be just time to catch a Bangkok flight, change, and connect with a Thai Airline plane to Singapore. Susan was waiting in a taxi with our luggage as I dashed from the weighing room after winning the last at Sha Tin. The traffic was desperate as usual but the driver, who doubled as a mafoo (stable lad) in the early morning, was no mug at the wheel and we made it with three minutes to spare.

So far so good. There should now be plenty of time to make the Singapore connection on arrival at Bangkok. And there was.

We presented our tickets for the second leg of the flight at check-in feeling confident of being ahead of schedule. The official at

Thailand's major airport examined our documents and nodded his head gravely. There was, he regretted, a slight delay. Thai had only recently been granted a route out of London. Had they lost their way?, I wondered. Whether or not they had taken the wrong course was not revealed during a courteously delivered, unenthusiastically received announcement which informed passengers to Singapore that a delay of seventeen hours was envisaged. There was nothing for it but to collect our baggage, book into a hotel for the night and hope that the interrupted service might yet be resumed in time for us to make it.

The following morning fog became a further obstacle. At the airport an indication of added delay shortened tempers and lengthened the odds. When we finally cleared the runway the time factor was critical. We'd be landing at Changi, the traditional crossroads for flights to and from Europe, during the rush hour. Passport control could be crowded, and as we were seated in the middle of the plane I was badly drawn for a fast exit. We rang for a steward to explain the problem. He didn't appear to understand much English and certainly didn't understand me. So I said to Susan, 'You're better at this than I am, you try him.' Susan gave him a sweet smile and explained: 'My husband is Lester Piggott. It is a matter of great urgency that he reaches the racecourse, where he is riding today within minutes of touchdown . . .'. She continued bravely until it became clear that she might have been speaking Swahili. The steward made soothing gestures, smiled nervously, and left us.

I'd got a set of gear in the weighing room at Bukit Timah, whose racecourse manager Tim Thompson had promised a car, with engine running, at the airport exit. We decided that Susan would bring the hand luggage and collect the cases while I made a dash for Immigration. I'd crept up to the front of the plane while it was taxiing and, first out of the stalls, raced for the Clearance Counter. There was a queue off another flight longer than any you've ever seen at the pari-mutuel at Longchamp on Arc day.

So I kept running. Through an unmanned Immigration gate. Through Customs, out into the main concourse. Peter O'Sullevan wrote in *Calling the Horses* that, 'By the time he [Lester] had won his first apprentice title at the age of fifteen, Keith and Iris Piggott's only son had collected more "yellow cards" than most of his contemporaries would gather in a lifetime.' Right now there were little yellow men popping up everywhere, running and shouting. It was like Keystone Cops in the Orient. The driver of the racecourse executive car waved and I called 'Go!', jumping in and lying on the floor as we exited from Changi airport.

Susan meanwhile had cleared Customs and travelled via our hotel to the racecourse, arriving in time to hear that I had won the first and to be confronted by an old friend who just happened to be Head of Security. He appeared deeply concerned and was accompanied by three young Chinese in uniform, two men and a woman. Their mission was to apprehend me forthwith and take me downtown for questioning on suspicion of illegal entry to Singapore. Another yellow card loomed!

It was one hour to post time for the big one when a formal meeting was convened in the Clerk of the Course's office and a compromise was reached. I could finish the afternoon at the track provided I reported to Immigration Headquarters first thing the following morning, when my fate would be determined.

My horse in the Lion City Cup needed to be held up but he had a good turn of foot. He used it inside the distance and just got up to win nicely. (Maybe the Immigration officials had invested a Singapore dollar or two, because the next day, after a severe reprimand, the matter was closed.)

'I thought for a moment you'd left it too late,' said the owner. 'So did I,' I told him.

Lester Piggott rode his first winner at the age of 12 in 1948, and was Champion Jockey 11 times between 1960 and 1982. He rode the winner of the Derby nine times, and his tally of 29 English Classic wins is a record.

Vincent O'Brien
LESTER TAKES THE MILE

I first met Lester Piggott at Cheltenham in the mid-Fifties, but it was not until 1958 that he rode for me. Gladness was the first in a string of successful partnerships; she won the Ascot Gold Cup, the Goodwood Cup and the Ebor Handicap by six lengths carrying top weight.

During the early Sixties, Lester was retained by Noel Murless and did the majority of his riding for him. Then in 1966 he won the Oaks on Valoris for me and in 1967 teamed up with the horse that Lester still maintains is the best he ever sat on, Sir Ivor, to win the Grand Criterium. The following year Sir Ivor collected the Two Thousand Guineas, Derby and Champion Stakes before going on to Washington to win the International, the first major American victory by a European horse. Nijinsky followed in 1970, Roberto in 1972, The Minstrel in 1977 and Alleged in 1977 and 1978. This list leaves out numerous top-class horses, but all were ridden with the distinctive Piggott panache and it is very doubtful whether anyone else would have won at Epsom on Roberto or The Minstrel.

After we split in 1980, I retained Pat Eddery, Cash Asmussen and John Reid during the following decade. Never did I think Lester and I would be back together again, but it's strange the way things happen!

When Lester set up as a trainer I felt it was not what really interested him. Yet I had known Susan, a daughter of Sam Armstrong, as a young girl; I had watched her set off for boarding school with the form-book under her arm and seen her instructing apprentices in her father's yard. I felt that training was bred in her bones.

In July 1990 my son-in-law John Magnier told me that he had met Lester recently and asked him how he spent his days. Lester said he rode out in the mornings and watched racing on SIS (on television) in the afternoons. John said, 'Why don't you start race riding again?'

and added, 'You think about it.' I rang Lester in August and said what John had told me and how about it? He said 'I'll give it some thought.' I rang him again a few weeks later and we arranged to meet in Dublin in September. I booked a private room for lunch in the Berkeley Court to avoid publicity. It was then that he said he would ride again.

I told Lester that I would give him first choice of mounts on my horses in 1991. My retained jockey in 1990 was John Reid. John broke his collarbone at Longchamp the first week in October and this put him out of action for the remainder of the season. I had four runners at the Curragh on 23 October and I asked Lester to come and ride. The meeting was a new one, specially scheduled to add some badly needed two-year-old races to the programme. I was running three two-year-olds and one three-year-old and while I thought they all had a chance, I hardly expected what followed. The first won comfortably; the second fairly easily; the third needed all the assistance Lester could give to get up by a short head and when the fourth horse pulled clear in the final furlong, the reception in the stands and when he returned to the winner's enclosure was tremendous. While some sceptics remained, many questions had been answered.

On 27 October, Royal Academy was engaged in the Breeder's Cup Mile at Belmont Park. Lester had approached me during the October Sales at Newmarket a few weeks previously and said that he would be delighted to ride the horse if I wanted. With John Reid out, I had offers from several other top jockeys: Steve Cauthen and Willie Carson in England and Pat Day and Angel Cordero from America. However, after consultation with the board of Classic Thoroughbreds, I decided to let Lester have the ride, confident in the knowledge that Royal Academy was exactly his type of horse. This decision was announced during the Sales and caused a considerable stir; I don't want to mention names, but several racing 'experts' questioned the wisdom of the move!

Unfortunately, I was unable to go to New York for the race owing to a bout of 'flu, but I knew that nothing would be left to chance by my staff or by Lester. This race was every bit as important to him as it was to me and he travelled out a day early in order to sit up on the horse on the morning before the race and also to walk the track.

His instructions on the day were simple; although Royal Academy had won the July Cup, he was not an out-and-out sprinter and didn't like to be put on top of his head coming out of the stalls.

So I told Lester to give him a chance to find his feet for the first furlong or so and not to worry about what was going on in front of him, as the pace was bound to be suicidal. He was drawn on the rail, a good position for a front-running type, but less than ideal for a horse who liked to sit off the pace.

The pre-race arrangements went perfectly; the horse travelled out on the Thursday on his own specially chartered plane. Lester gave him a canter on the sand training track on the Friday and confirmed that he was in good order. Royal Academy took the preliminaries very well – the parade ring in Belmont was unbridled chaos with photographers and television crews everywhere, but both horse and rider seemed unperturbed. The field was loaded in order of post position, meaning that we went in first. Perhaps as a result of being in for some time, Royal Academy broke slowly enough and was at least a length last after a furlong. As expected, the pace was very strong for the first half mile and Lester was content to make gradual progress up the outside, leaving him in about seventh position going into the home turn.

Coming out of the bend, Royal Academy just ducked towards the rail for a moment for no apparent reason. This caused him to lose momentum and very nearly cost him the race as it took valuable time for Lester to get him balanced and running again. He still had a good six lengths or so to make up and only a furlong and a half in which to do it; that they managed it at all was a tribute to both horse and rider. To tumultuous cheers from the packed grandstands, Royal Academy got his head in front on the line.

The scenes afterwards were unbelievable; everyone who had ever even set foot in Ireland gave themselves honorary Irishman status for the afternoon and arrived in the winner's enclosure. There were hardened racing veterans with tears in their eyes and the faxes and telephone messages started to come pouring into Ballydoyle. The racing world seemed to realize that something unique had happened that day. There's nothing worse than a revered sportsman who makes an unsuccessful comeback, but Lester, yet again, had proved everyone wrong. I am only glad that I had the opportunity to play a part in an occasion which will be remembered for many years.

Irish trainer Vincent O'Brien has made his mark on the racing world with successes in the Grand National (three times), the Champion Hurdle (three times), the Cheltenham Gold Cup (four times) the Epsom Derby (six times) and the Irish Derby (five times).

Peter O'Sullevan
THE BASTARD

In November 1964 I flew to Australia with Scobie Breasley, described by the legendary twenty-eight times British champion Sir Gordon Richards as 'one of the all-time greats in the history of the game'.

Arthur Edward Breasley, whose nickname derived from a highly successful old-time Aussie trainer Jim Scobie, was a household name in his native land in the fifties when he was lured to England by the bluff millionaire miller James Rank. Having intended to stay for a season he was now returning 'home' for the first time in a decade, four times British champion jockey and winner, as a 50-year-old grandfather, of that year's Derby on Santa Claus. He had been invited by the Victoria Racing Club to take part as an honoured guest in the renowned Racing Festival which featured the Melbourne Cup – the richest race prize in the southern hemisphere and the greatest traffic-stopper in the sporting world – and the Victoria Derby, the oldest established race in Australia. From the moment the Qantas Boeing 707 came under orders at Heathrow and well-iced vodka was being served with unstinting helpings of Beluga caviar, Wagga Wagga's most famous son was treated with the reverence of a cherished national idol.

On the last lap of a long flight, having switched from champagne to Bordeaux with his duck and later declined a second Pêche Melba, Scobie calculated on the back of the menu that since his first win at Werribee in 1928 he'd lost three-and-a-half tons.

He explained, 'I've been riding for thirty-six years and I take off a minimum of 1lb a day – up to three on a hot day – during a programme. So at an average of 150 days' race-riding a year and allowing for 1½lb sweated away each time, that is 8,100lb.'

An impressive statistic but not at all exceptional in a sustained

106

riding career. What was unusual was the detail that the homeward-bound cavalier could go to scale at 8 stone in colours without ever undertaking any exhausting artificial weight reduction. So that, for all his mileage, Scobie was like a lightly raced horse. A Classic one.

My assignment was to file each day to the *Daily Express* copy which would be reproduced in the *Melbourne Herald,* and to move on from Australia to report the clash between US equine stars Kelso and Gun Bow, among others, in the Washington International at Laurel. It seemed improbable, Scobie agreed, that the Committee would have invited him to take part in the great Festival without pre-arranging partners in both the Derby and Cup – the latter being the only major event on the Australasian continent he had not yet won. But, so far, he had no indication of any booking. The quest resulted in one of the most uncanny experiences of my racing life – and one that could scarcely be told in detail at the time.

Meanwhile, in the fast-fading light, we were about to land. As the Boeing lost height the cluster of phosphorescent amber rectangles which carpeted the landscape turned into floodlit tennis courts –just as, a week later, the brilliant emeralds beneath the night sky of Los Angeles became swimming pools. With nearly forty-eight hours to go Melbourne was firmly in the grip of Festival fever. There was just time to check into the Southern Cross, bathe and change before a reception and dinner after which I still appeared to be preoccupied with bestowing fervent support on the wine growers of Hunter Valley when it was time to watch morning track work.

Everywhere the unanswered question was the same: 'What will Scobie ride in the Derby and Cup?' Everywhere in this vibrant city of three million souls and nearly that many punters there was an air of buoyant expectancy – heightened this year by the prosperity conferred on the Australian Turf by TAB, the brainchild of former VRC chairman Sir Chester Manifold. Initiated in 1961 to the accompaniment of widespread prophecies of failure, the Totalisator Agency Board's object was to provide a service to off-course punters, from whom the tracks would receive a percentage of the money staked – leaving the bookmakers, whose off-course activity had been made illegal, to continue to provide a colourful and strong market on the racetracks. The race clubs put up the initial £600,000 operational costs with the enlightened government agreeing to take a 3 per cent clip rising to 4 per cent if and when the outlay had been recovered. By 1964 there were 126 shops in and around Melbourne. But what a contrast to their British counterparts, featuring running commentaries, betting 'shows', instant pay-out, etc. . . . little wonder that their failure was so widely forecast.

Amenities have been modified since. However, when I visited a TAB in the Victoria capital's Plaza precinct, hoping for entertainment and possible improvement of my financial status, I found that all 'investments' (in five-shilling units) had to be made forty minutes before the 'off'; running commentaries and the carrying of transistors were forbidden; no results were posted until the following day, and no pay-out entertained until then. And yet from modest beginnings the 1963–4 official report revealed the citizenry of Victoria to have invested £40,593,708. No wonder that when I drove fifty miles north to Kyneton, almost leaving the road at my first sight of a brilliantly coloured flight of budgerigars, the small, lively, up-country meeting had big rebuilding plans due to their cut of the day's shop take. As I write that was twenty-seven years ago. Imagine what Plumpton, similarly resourced, would look like now!

Back in town there was a chat show request (everyone who was anybody and anybody who was nobody, which let me in, was being interviewed) and a message from Scobie about a dinner that night and would I like to go to Caulfield in the morning when he was to work a potential Derby ride?

The matter of Scobie's participation in Derby and Cup had become an embarrassing issue. While his hosts hoped very much that he would be in action they had no jurisdiction over the owners and trainers involved. The racing game is as tough as it is sentimental and the fact was that there was no stampede to unship tried and regular partners in favour of a 50-year-old grandad who (some argued) might well be ring-rusty round the uniform tight home circuit.

The trainer we went to see, Charlie Sanderson, was one of the old school and understood the full worth of the services of Arthur Edward Breasley. After we'd been introduced and watched Bering Strait (a son of 1957 Eclipse winner, Arctic Explorer) and Scobie set off in the early morning light on the sand track, he said, 'This'll interest you. I've asked the "old fellow" to come six furlongs in even time [fifteen seconds to the furlong]. He won't have done this for a long while. We'll see how much he's forgotten.'

At each marker the handler of Bering Strait, who had won his maiden nicely and seemed a progressive sort, pressed his stopwatch and showed it to me. The pilot, who had the previous evening taken aboard enough liquor to float the Queen Mary, was spot-on – not one-hundredth of a second out. It was some sort of miracle.

Scobie didn't seem to want to hang about after riding work. He told the trainer he'd see him at the track in the afternoon and we went to the car. I asked him if he'd been counting to arrive at such precision timing. No, he hadn't given it a thought. He'd been asked to come even time, so he came even time. That was all there was to it.

We'd been driving a little while when Scobie said, 'I won't be riding that horse.' I was surprised – for the second time that morning. Had he got an alternative possibility? No, he hadn't. 'But,' he said, 'I'd rather be in the stands than have him.'

We were both feeling a little delicate after sufficient overnight intake of the excellent local claret to discourage small talk on the following morning. But there had to be a story here. Everyone knew that his prospective Cup mount, Gold Chick, had as much chance of winning as Keith Miller had of being named misogamist of the year. But this was a very different proposition – as the betting reflected.

'What's wrong with him?' I asked.

'I don't know,' replied my fellow traveller, 'but he's a bastard.' Enquiry among colleagues, including that regular visitor to England, Jack Elliott, throughout the Flemington press room, yielded no stain on Bering Strait's character. Nor were there grounds for questioning his ancestry. Impressed by the manner in which he had won a maiden as part of the build-up to what would be the richest ever Victoria Derby, there were race-writers and radio reporters who would nominate the Breasley reject as good value. But Scobie, son of a sheep drover and trainer of trotters, had literally ridden before he could walk. Somehow his sensitive horseman's hands had picked up an alien vibration.

The topless fashion was in vogue in 1964 and the warm spring afternoon of 1 November had encouraged distracting degrees of exposure among several visitors to the premier Classic – notably a strikingly statuesque brunette who wore nothing but extravagantly wide-mesh netting between a becomingly broad-brimmed black hat and skirt, and whose viewing position adjacent to the press balcony challenged the concentration of the most dedicated student of race form. Nevertheless, as the last of the Derby runners entered the stalls – which had yet to be introduced in England – few can have missed the early drama as Bering Strait dived across the horse on his inside, pitched, and gave his rider, Ian Saunders, a crashing fall.

Scobie knew I'd be late back to the car park because I had copy to write as usual. When we finally met up he was drinking with friends in the evening sun, having been to commiserate with the injured jock. He filled me a glass of cool champagne, raised his glass and smiled.

'I told you that horse was a bastard!'

Peter O'Sullevan is a racing journalist and commentator: Press Association 1944–50; Daily Express 1950–86; BBC 1946– . Author of racing autobiography, Calling the Horses. *Director, International Racing Bureau and* Racing Post. *OBE 1977, CBE 1991. Elected to the Jockey Club 1987. Patron, International League for the Protection of Horses and Brooke Hospital for Animals.*

Foreign fields

Hugh McIlvanney
THAT GOLDEN GLOW

My favourite tribute to the restorative value of a day at the races occurred at the end of a fairly harrowing television documentary about an American lawyer's struggle to save a young convict from execution. There was a strong case for commuting the death sentence but the campaign suffered from the reluctance of public figures to risk identifying with the cause. Politicians and religious leaders first pledged support and then ducked out under pressure. But the lawyer had brains and heart and stamina and in the end he got a result.

When word of the victory came through, he was exultant, but euphoria was followed by a predictable reaction. Suddenly he looked lost; spiritually drained but left with a reservoir of adrenalin that was now surplus to requirements. Then, brightening abruptly, he shouted to one of his assistants: 'Go down and get me a scratch sheet – I'm going to the track.' And the last shot we saw of him was through the window of a race train. He was scrutinizing the scratch sheet (which is an up-to-date list of runners) and the expression on his face showed that he was being transported in more ways than one.

Some people, adapting the late Bill Shankly's famous line about football, might suggest that our man was leaving behind matters of life and death and heading towards something more important. It is true that among some of the betting men I have accompanied into the fray, a day at the track has often seemed as relaxing as a picnic in an air-raid. But, for most of us occasional jousters in the ring, racing remains just about the most irresistible form of communal escapism civilized (well, comparatively civilized) man has yet devised. The racecourse is a place where everyday reality is suspended in favour of a theatrically heightened version. Being there is, for us if not for the professionals, like experiencing one of those dreams in which we are exposed to all sorts of crises and excitements, dramas and dangers, but can wake up unscathed. Obviously if the betting arm is allowed to get out of control reality of the old-fashioned kind may reassert itself jarringly by way of the bailiffs or the chaps with bent noses. Given a reasonable grip on the fantasies, however, we have a licence to enjoy thousands of adventure playgrounds scattered about the globe.

Many are memorably beautiful. At such places as Goodwood, Chantilly, Santa Anita and Gulfstream the eye is given so much pleasure that impoverishment seems almost a privilege. Now and again, I admit, it is hard to concentrate on the glories of the scenery when the bankroll is being amputated, with or without the aid of anaesthetic. An afternoon at a track outside Caracas, Venezuela, comes to mind. It offered unforgettable views towards distant mountains but not a glimpse of a winner – and, unless the memory has been distorted by trauma, there were twelve races on the card. At least I lasted the distance and lost a lot less painfully than Ken Norton, whose attempt to take the world heavyweight champion-ship from the young George Foreman was the justification for my presence in Venezuela. Poor Norton was frightened into impotence in the first round and battered away from his senses in the second.

I have suffered the punter's equivalent of a knockout at racecourses on several continents. There have also been occasions when the contest has been stopped to save the bank manager from further punishment and, let's own up, one or two cases in which the towel has been tossed into the ring. But recuperation is invariably swift and the next time the bell rings I am usually eager to answer it. That is especially true in Australia, where finding something to bet on is as easy as falling off a cliff. I recall a day in 1983 when the drop towards the breadline was made in company that was interesting then and is even more so in retrospect. Included in our group was Mick Channon. At that time Mick was still a professional footballer with Norwich City and had taken his boots to New South Wales to earn a bit of extra money before the start of another English season. You will have noticed that of late his name (more formally presented as M. Channon, Upper Lambourn) has been appearing fairly frequently in race results columns in the space reserved for the winning trainer.

By 1983 Mick, whose speed and scoring capacity made him an exciting member of the England team in his prime, was already heavily committed to the breeding of horses and there were clear signs that his second career was likely to be concerned with racing rather than football. But our mutual experience of the Warwick Farm track on the outskirts of Sydney was liable to cause him to think again. We suffered uninterrupted devastation, in spite of Mick's attempt to combat our ignorance of local form by enlisting one of his pals as reader of the runes. Chris Docherty was a transplanted Derryman who worked with Australian Telecom but once inside the purlieus of a racecourse he did not behave much like a wage-earner. I noted at the time that when the mood was on him (which meant when the cash was on him) he performed like a scaled-down replica of J. P. McManus, the Limerick Leviathan. Buoyed up by a profitable outing at a country meeting earlier in the week, Docherty arrived at Warwick Farm anxious to try the best of three falls with the bookies. He in fact took eight falls in a row – a number dictated by the fact that we ran out of races – and we tourists went down with his tattered banner.

Even the names of our losers seemed to mock us. Bistro Star was a flop, Fast Food was too slow and Obey didn't. It was a glorious afternoon, with a pale sun shining on cool vistas of trees and grass and rainbow silks, but in a punting sense it was Gallipoli and we were resigned long before somebody nearby said of one of our selections that 'it couldn't run out of sight in the dark'. Yet the mood of retreat could not survive the quietly hilarious trip back to Sydney. Race trains, like troop trains, are always heading for the next battle. In a couple of days they would be running the Brisbane Cup in sunny Queensland and there would be a chance for revenge. Astonishingly, I took it. The tough staying five-year-old Amarant had recently won the Adelaide Cup and was joint favourite for the big 3,200-metre race at Eagle Farm in Brisbane, but backable at 11–2. When Amarant overcame the trouble created by a collision that put two of his rivals on the floor, and surged beyond the other faltering competitors like a motor-cyclist accelerating through roller-skaters, Australian racing's hold on the affections of this visitor was unbreakable.

A week later, with the theatre of hostilities shifted to Victoria, I flew 200 miles west of Melbourne to follow the fortunes of Brent

Thomson (a rider not unknown to British racegoers) amid the rural delights of Warrnambool Racing Club, which is enough of a 'bush' track to make Wincanton look like Longchamp. That day I was combining the functions of journalist, punter and part-time valet. I gained admission by humping a saddle from the taxi to the jockeys' room. So well did Thomson look after our interests out on the course, I'd have been happy to carry the saddle with him sitting in it. Flying back to Melbourne through the unforgettable beauty of a Victorian sunset, in the seat beside the pilot of a tiny Cessna, was blissful and the rapture was not diminished by the fact that the young man in the back had just ridden the last Warrnambool winner at 6–1. Brent's in Hong Kong these days. Why can't Don King arrange for a heavyweight title fight out there?

Of course, the joys of the track are just as likely to be found on your own doorstep as on the other side of the world. No sporting arena anywhere has brought me a greater volume of pleasure over the last thirty years than Cheltenham, though it is a corner of the Cotswolds in which I have coped with more vicissitudes than John Bunyan's pilgrim. The sheer bulk and diversity of my experiences there stifle the temptation to go into detail. The drinks bill alone, if collected and bound, would provide a book to make Jeffrey Archer's latest look like a pocket diary. It might be a better read, too, especially the parts that would come across in an Irish accent.

National Hunt racing has always been a reliable source of special moments and you don't have to go to either of the two principal shrines of the jumping game, Cheltenham and Aintree, to prove the point. Plumpton will do when the human cast includes men as appealing as the youthful Josh Gifford I went to interview on an afternoon I can still remember vividly two-and-a-half decades on. Josh rode four winners on that programme but the fear of jinxing him kept me off all of them. It is not, however, the memory of costly altruism that stays with me most vibrantly, nor even that of the enjoyable evening we had in Findon afterwards. It is the recollection of a brave and brilliant jockey's thoughts as he steered his Mercedes through the Sussex lanes in the dusk of that February day in 1967. 'God, I need a fall,' he said earnestly. 'I'm really due one. I haven't come off since Hello Dolly the day after Boxing Day. I must have gone more than sixty rides without one. I want one badly.'

From a man who, in the years before that drive, had come off horses heavily enough to break his neck, his leg, his nose, his cheekbone, his wrist, his ribs, his fingers and a few other bones, it was a slightly unexpected remark. He was prepared to elaborate. 'I'd like one fall a week. Not a bad one to hurt myself. Just to feel myself sliding along the grass and then get up and give myself a shake and say, "Well that's that. I've had my fall and now I can get on with it." But when you haven't had one for a while you begin to wait for it to happen, and it can affect the way you ride, maybe even cause you to come off when it wasn't absolutely necessary. I don't mean you're out there looking to fall. But you may go into a fence just a little wrong and you say to yourself, "Ooh! Here it comes" – whereas if you have had your fall recently you say "Get on! Get over, you bastard." '

Josh got his fall soon enough, and plenty of others. But he kept getting up to thrill us again. He is still doing it as a trainer.

I have never had a horse in training with Josh, or anyone else come to that (the brief leasing of a two-year-old called Towering Ambition scarcely counts, since no amount of ambition could sustain that one's undoubted speed more than a few yards beyond four furlongs). But don't imagine that I have been denied the pleasures of ownership. They were mine for a day and it may have been the most satisfying I have known on the racecourse. There should be no sniggering at the back when I acknowledge that the racecourse in question was Ludlow.

The dream day came when two friends of mine who owned a workmanlike novice hurdler called Overall found they could not make it to Shropshire for a race in which he was strongly fancied. My credentials for being elected surrogate owner were limited to a mild fondness for quoting A. E. Housman's *A Shropshire Lad*, but I got the job. I think I did so because my friends reckoned that my late betting advice from the course had to be more enlightening than the mass of bewildering testimony conveyed on an earlier occasion by another member of our circle. He had so baffled Overall's connections with his detailed analysis that they had finished up wagering against the four-year-old, who responded appropriately to their defection by winning as he liked. I promised to be more decisive, even if it meant being decisively wrong.

As I set out with a couple of allies on the expedition to Ludlow, our main concern was the going we would find there. Overall did not like the firm. His prejudice dominated conversation all the way up through the West Country and as we parked on the course my eagerness to be reassured on this vital issue undid my attempts to play the laid-back owner. I was testing the ground before I was halfway out of the car. Finding my heel sinking in an inch or so, I was able to reclaim my air of composure. 'This will do us,' I said professionally. 'Yes,' said one of my companions, 'if they run the race through the car park he's a good thing.'

When I went to watch Overall being readied for his work, I felt they could run the race along the motorway and he would still be too much for the opposition. The little, light-framed horse stood with the dignity of a bullfighter being dressed for the ring while the saddle was strapped on him and the girths were tightened. He looked reserved, but no less confident than he had a right to be after winning the second of his two previous hurdle races by twelve lengths at Wincanton. The trainer, Les Kennard, was doing business at the Newmarket Sales but his wife, who was standing in for him at Ludlow, said Overall should be able to give weight and a beating to the eighteen moderate hurdlers against him. She gave his face a last wipe with a wet sponge, then squeezed it in his mouth. 'A drop of gin and tonic before you go,' she said with a laugh.

It was champagne we were drinking after Overall won so easily that the rather tight prices offered by the bookmakers began to look extravagant as he came over the last. The connections had made a concerted assault on the enemy. We took a little 2–1, a little 15–8 and a lot of 7–4 and left the masses with the evens. Driving into the dark of a November evening in England isn't quite the same as flying through an Australian sunset, but the two experiences can be linked by the glow that remains after a great day at the races.

Hugh McIlvanney writes for the Observer. *He is alone in having been named Sports Writer of the Year five times in the British Press Awards; in 1981 he was voted Journalist of the Year.*

Richard Pitman
THE DUELING GROUNDS

Kentucky, Bluegrass country, $750,000: the inaugural running of the Dueling Grounds Hurdle was just too tasty to miss so I set off into the unknown with an open mind, paying my own expenses and happy that April Fools' Day had been three weeks earlier.

Shopping around secured a ticket for just £300; I thought of letting Barry Hills and Robert Sangster know, then aborted the idea as they must surely be ahead of the game by now! Such indeed turned out to be the case: the world's biggest jumping prize plus the probable sale of Nomadic Way afterwards prompted the dynamic duo to catch Concorde.

Heathrow to Washington, no trouble. Washington to Nashville, not quite so smooth! After two hours of airport food we boarded what proved to be an overbooked flight; yet despite being squashed between an obese sweating man with wind problems (I do not mean his respiratory system) and his larger wife with a worse affliction of which her best friend had failed to inform her, I was stupid enough not to jump at the chance to accept an alternative flight with an extra stop. Two hours twenty minutes later, still sitting on the runway, the flight was abandoned due to the unwillingness of the port side engine to do anything more promising than the fat man. It was then that I found the catch to travelling on the cheap. The other passengers were accommodated for the night; I was told to return by 10 a.m. the next day. 'You're welcome' seemed inadequate really. The airport hotel was very nice but as it was then 11.30 p.m. the only room left was $200 which cancelled out the initial bargain and made Concorde look feasible. I don't expect American journalist Anne Barker, who waited four hours in vain to meet me at Nashville, was too thrilled either.

The racecourse, placed strategically just over the border from

119

Tennessee where betting was not allowed, was designed to attract the punters who wished to be clean at heart but have the facility to bet nearby. The lavish betting pavilion invited interested parties to dine well with unobtrusive television sets at every table in the most expensive areas. As the eating facilities became more affordable to the three-car family, so the TV monitors became larger.

The enterprise was the brainchild of former stable-hand Mike Shannon who had fought his way to the top, eventually owning the 1976 champion USA Flat racehorse Manila. Having seen the business of betting from the bottom up, Mike ensured patrons were accommodated at the twitch of an eyebrow by willing runners.

As with all new ventures, the vast pavilion was still being finished the day before the big race with an army of men carpeting and fixing huge interior windows into place with high velocity nail guns and huge staplers. Even though the place was being fixed, furnished and finished around them, there were plenty of betting-starved business men and indeed well-heeled families willing to get some action. When I say well-heeled I mean exactly that as we were in the heart of Cowboy Boot country and their occupants seemed intent on filling them with winnings via televised racing from other states.

One 20-stone, crew-cut, silk-suited punter had obviously been shot at numerous times before as his bulk was up and sprinting before his drink hit the table.

My tour of the building ended with a drink of fruit juice on the spacious balcony, the equivalent of our Members' stand.

The course below ran for about a mile and a quarter and was oval in shape with banked bends at both ends like a cycling track. The home turn was raised fully 17 feet from its lowest rail to the outside of the course. Even to a punchdrunk old cavalier like me it was immediately obvious that any horse racing high up would be subjecting its near foreleg to unreasonable strain; and so it proved.

On the plus side was a superb watering system which could cover the whole course with an inch of water in twenty minutes. This promoted lush grass, but sadly much of the banked part of the track had been eroded through flash floods prior to the ground settling and there were many bare patches, albeit concealed by a green-coloured mush. The state of the ground had caused the racing manager, Steve Groat, to voice his fears so strongly as to cause his replacement less than a week before the event. This mover and shaker, called 'Doc', roamed continuously in a Range Rover uttering a throaty growl.

All within the space of the final twenty-four hours car parks, parade ring, flower beds, temporary stands and food tents materialized on the scene with military precision.

Of the nine runners in the Dueling Grounds Hurdle, Paddy Mullins' Grabel, Barry Hills' Nomadic Way and Michael Robinson's Valrodian represented the UK while Peer Prince and Regal Ambition had been bought from English stables with this race in mind. The soft ground specialist Collins from France completed the foreign challenge, leaving the entire Uptown Swell and Jonathan Sheppard's pair Polar Pleasure and Summer Colony to defend the prize for the home side.

The Irish mare Grabel was last to arrive at the course, having endured the most gruelling journey by road from New York. She had taken the transatlantic flight in her dainty stride and despite being stuck in a typical New York rush hour traffic snarl-up, hopped out of her motorized prison as if the previous sixteen hours had been spent at a luxurious stud instead of on the road. This journey, plus the facts that the jumps were like point-to-point fences (she had only jumped hurdles beforehand) and jockey Tony Mullins had given up riding over fences himself years before, caused me to view the Irish team's blinding confidence with some scepticism.

Despite the arduous journey, trainer Paddy Mullins ordered an early evening schooling session for both the mare's and the jockey's benefit. Grabel respected the first jump while Tony entertained spectators with his impression of Brod Munro-Wilson.

By the next they were as smooth as Dunwoody and Nomadic Way, who had already caught the Americans' eye as the likely winners. Paddy Mullins grunted satisfaction and turned on his heel while part-owner Paddy Keogh tightened his grip on the huge roll of dollars he intended to invest twenty hours later and Maureen Mullins displayed a teasing grin that clearly said, 'All you journalists who wanted Tony's head in the Dawn Run saga may soon be eating your own newsprint!'

Michael Robinson had engaged local rider Chuck Lawrence to partner Valrodian and although the new pairing clicked, New Zealand's champion hurdler had not shone since he arrived to race in the northern hemisphere. The Martin Pipe-trained Regal

121

Ambition had the form, the scope and the looks to justify his reputed $300,000 price tag. Under the care of Pipe's assistant chirpy Chester Barnes, a personal vet and a pair of farriers plus his devoted handler Sarah, the winner of Cheltenham's novice hurdling championship was a worthy opponent for the more experienced Nomadic Way. Peer Prince, formerly trained in Newmarket and to be ridden here by the irrepressible Steve Smith Eccles, did not look good enough on paper to win but had the form to have a bite at it. Of the home team, the entire Uptown Swell partnered by the teenage student Blythe Miller was most interesting. A good stakes winner on the flat, he had been kept in training for a hurdling career instead of a pampered life at stud by his sporting owner Virginia Kraft Payson who reasoned: 'I have racehorses for fun and a career at stud would be more fun for the horse than for me.'

Race day was very hot. The limos ejected their tanned occupants, lunch parties excitedly claimed a stake in their fancy for the world's richest jump race and flat jockey Randy Romero looked at his jumping counterparts as if they were freaks. Open-air viewing boxes in tiers adjacent to the wire (finish) had all been sold to the sporting families who had turned out from South Carolina, Kentucky, Maryland and Virginia. Over there, support means exactly that.

The parade ring, which had received its final coat of paint only hours earlier, was adorned by an abundance of flowers hired for the day, and the rolls of turf laid for the occasion did the job of supporting the throng of connections. An unusual mix of expensive perfume and suntan oil added to sweat and leather produced an air that was special to the day. Those few hours of sport were the minimum legal requirement needed to provide the course's betting parlour with a reason to exist.

Scanning the runners it seemed to me that Regal Ambition and Nomadic Way would have most to fear from Summer Colony and Uptown Swell; but I have been known to be wrong in the past too. The excitement of the occasion even got to the normally reticent Martin Pipe, who let me have £100 of the bet he had struck in Ireland prior to jetting out. 'I doubt if the money will get back to this course to spoil the price,' he proffered.

Although the nine runners set off tightly bunched, Tony Mullins rightly had a feeler on Grabel over the first three jumps. Having got

the right vibrations, he moved the mare nearer the front to cover
Jonathan Lower on the pacemaker Regal Ambition, who he knew
would have the ability to stay in front and even quicken to boot. The
mix of American, French, Irish and British horses, jockeys, owners,
trainers and supporters burst into a spontaneous reaction as the
field passed the stands with cheers loud enough to galvanize even
the faintest heart. But there were none in this contest. Fast, even
breathtaking leaps were asked for and received when they sped
down the back stretch with Regal Ambition holding the pack at
bay. The bet looked good. As they climbed the final banked bend
between the third and second last jumps the pursuers, led by Grabel,
swallowed the long-time leader up, to the disbelief of those who
know that Pipe horses usually find another gear when tackled. As
with all races, thoughts for a runner only dwell while it is in
contention; so allegiance leapfrogged to Grabel who within
seconds, having been Irish up to that point, became British.

Swooping down the bank into the short straight with only two
jumps between him and victory, Tony Mullins was not going to be
denied. Riding as if his father were firing buckshot at his backside,
he drove the mare at the final obstacles as if they were figments of
the public imagination.

The line crossed, it seemed that half the huge American crowd
suddenly remembered long-forgotten Irish antecedents; or perhaps
there is a simpler explanation, that they had enjoyed a truly
multinational race.

Blythe Miller, looking every inch a jockey, conjured a late run
from Uptown Swell to be second with Colvin Ryan third on Polar
Pleasure and Steve Smith Eccles getting the best out of Peer Prince in
fourth. In the heat of the victory presentations few noticed Regal
Ambition being led back having broken down on both forelegs,
despite passing previous vet tests including tendon scans.

As with the Seagram Grand National meeting, supporting races
do not exist for winning teams. The unfaltering confidence of owner
Paddy Keogh saw the arrival of a pickup truck with two plastic
laundry baskets filled with ice and alcoholic drinks – in a dry
county!

Even though the whole show had been staged to satisfy the legal
conditions for betting, the jumping world responded as never
before: money is obviously the key to promoting international jump

racing. Few who were in Kentucky for that race will forget the occasion – including Grabel, who is now enjoying the spicier side of the game at stud.

Richard Pitman failed his 9 'O' Levels, which directly led him to a life in racing stables. After 15 seasons as a jump jockey (470 winners, 5000 losers), he retired in 1975 to join the BBC Television team for the steeplechase season. He is a weekly contributor to the Sunday Express.

Peter Willett
BEATING ABOUT THE BUSH

There are 128 racecourses in New South Wales staging 1,142 race days a year; a prodigious volume of racing for a state with eight million inhabitants. Apart from the metropolitan courses in the interminable urban sprawl of Sydney, racing takes place on so-called 'bush' courses ranging the full north–south length of the state. Bush meetings are run under state rules, with professional trainers, jockeys, stipendaries, swab stewards, race-callers and Australian Jockey Club-appointed handicappers. The races are started from stalls, and there is a photo-finish camera. Nevertheless, the atmosphere of a bush meeting partakes of much of the relaxed nature of an English point-to-point.

Bush meetings do not come any bushier than Bowraville, home of the Nambucca River Jockey Club 250 miles north of Sydney. To the casual eye Bowraville is the model of a one-horse town, consisting of little more than a single street of bungalows set in small gardens behind white picket fences, a couple of pubs, a shop or two, a church, a bank and a restaurant. In the midday heat there is hardly a sign of a soul stirring, but appearances are notoriously deceptive. Beneath this tranquil surface, they say, there is much bad blood between the white and the aboriginal communities; in February 1991 three aboriginal children went missing, and one of them was found murdered out in the bush.

None of this racial tension was apparent at Bowraville racecourse on Saturday 9 March that year, 'International Rugby Race Day', when the races were named after Australian rugger stars and the brothers Gary and Glen Ella graced the occasion with their presence. The scene is a seemingly undisturbed pastoral paradise, with the almost circular 1,200-metre course set in a bowl of well-treed parkland. A stand of graceful casuarinas and their feathery

125

evergreen foliage shades the entrance gate, where a man in a brick sentry-box collects the admission charge of $4 (£1.73). You park where you please for no charge. There is no grandstand, but that does not matter, because the bank which rings that side of the bowl is a natural viewing point, giving a clear panorama of the whole circuit. The sun was fierce, the temperature in the high eighties, and the crowd picnicked happily on sandwiches and lamertons (sponge cake sprinkled with coconut) under brightly coloured umbrellas. At the top of the bank there were a dozen wooden benches and tables, and by the end of the afternoon the table tops were invisible under serried ranks of empty beer 'tinnies' and 'stubbies', with all the sward around them marvellously free of litter. Bush racegoers are a tidy breed. Toddlers toddled, and babies crawled, suckled and had sodden nappies changed, innocently oblivious of the sporting and gambling environment.

For it is where the gambling starts that the point-to-point atmosphere ends. The betting facilities, indeed, are sophisticated. Under the octagonal timber roofs of two open-sided barns television screens display the latest betting fluctuations at the metropolitan meetings in Sydney, Melbourne, Brisbane and Adelaide, and another screen shows the principal races at those meetings live. Fully computerized betting on all the races at the metropolitan meetings, as well as the local races, is available at any of the six windows at the brick Tote building. In addition half a dozen bookmakers offer odds displayed on huge boards on each race at the metropolitan meetings, and six more bet on the Bowraville races. No off-course money comes back to the pools on the Bowraville races, and the course market is so weak that some weird distortions and variations result from quite small wagers. Ever So Vain, the pillar-to-post winner of the opening Will Ofahenague Maiden Handicap, started at 6–1 with the bookmakers and paid 17–1 for a win on the Tote; and Konkaroo, the easy winner of the Glen Ella Class 4 Handicap, paid only marginally less for a place than he did for a win on the Tote.

The jockeys may be bush specialists but they attain a high degree of competence, sitting in close to their horses and keeping them very straight under pressure. Races are run at a scorching pace round the constant bends; the straight is less than a furlong and the runners thunder to the line six abreast in a cloud of dust. The horses are not

126

the cream of the thoroughbred population, but equally they are not donkeys. They covered 1,000 metres in less than 59 seconds, and that cannot be bad. Mark Time had broken 1 minute 10 seconds when winning his previous race over 1,200 metres, and on this occasion he came from way back to win over 1,300 metres going away in record time of 1 minute 17.2 seconds. He looked a good sprinter. A man wearing a grey straw trilby and a gravely judicial air told me: 'He'll win in Sydney.' I could believe him.

Some of the horses were by highly reputable stallions. Fortitude, winner of the Nambucca Valley Rugby Open Handicap, was by Imperial Prince, whose grandson Tierce two weeks later won Australia's joint richest race, the Tooheys Golden Slipper Stakes, and went on to achieve the rare feat of winning the Sydney juvenile Triple Crown. Other Nambucca Valley Rugby Handicap runners were by the top speed stallion Biscay and Whiskey Road, sire of the globe-trotting Australian horse Strawberry Road.

Prize money is minimal. We hear a great deal about the staggeringly high prize money scales in Australia, and that is true enough at the metropolitan courses. Two weeks later at Rosehill (Sydney) the Golden Slipper Stakes was worth A$2m and the 'BMW' was worth A$1m; the least valuable race on the eight-race card was worth A$50,000. In the bush it is quite otherwise. The Bowraville races were worth a risible A$1,600 each, of which A$1,150 (about £500) went to the winner. With some horses boxed 100 miles to the meeting, there is not much profit in it for owners even if they do have a win. Owners with runners at Bowraville are racing strictly for sport and fun; and Bowraville racing is fun.

The betting barns are not the only buildings on Bowraville racecourse. There is a bar, a hamburger stand, a weighing room and a jockeys' changing room, and a photo-finish tower incorporating a balcony for the Stewards and the race commentator, the tower being constructed of green painted clapboard. The Stipe is less well provided for. He has to climb a rickety ladder to a scaffolded platform at the head of the straight for every race, but on 9 March his lack of amenities was compensated for by an absence of the stress and strain normally inseparable from his professional duties. Although there were fifty-three runners in five races on the cramped track, there was not a single objection or enquiry, nor anything else to disturb his peaceful contemplation of the pastoral scene.

Tinnies and stubbies of Tooheys are a bargain A$2 each wherever you buy them, but when it came to my turn to buy a round I was advised to boycott the bar and go to the window in a brick annexe attached to the Tote building, where the beer was cooler. When I got there I saw why. Inside the annexe hundreds of stubbies were stacked in a rusty old steel bath full of cracked ice standing on the concrete floor. The salesmen were two grave middle-aged gentlemen in dark suits and trilbies. The beer was in perfect condition.

Racing is nothing if not elitist. The best horses should win most money in open competition on the fairest tracks. By that strict criterion, Rosehill is at the heart and Bowraville is on the periphery of racing in New South Wales. But Bowraville, and other courses like it, have their proper place in the overall Australian social and sporting scheme of things. Bowraville, with the beauty of its setting beneath a wide burnished sky, the determination of its jockeys and sweating thoroughbreds on that headlong downhill charge to the finishing line, its race-caller chattily discussing the probabilities on the public address system during the wait for a photo-finish result, its juxtaposition of the intimacy and informality of its picnics with the sophistication of its betting set-up, its tidily marshalled tinnies and stubbies, has a special, enveloping, irresistible charm that I shall never forget.

Peter Willett has written a number of books about racing and breeding, the latest being A History of the General Stud Book. *He is a director of the National Stud and Goodwood racecourse, and chairman of the Trustees of the British European Breeders' Fund.*

The return of the maestro: Lester Piggott enters the paddock at Leicester for his first mount in Britain since 29 October 1985

Peter O'Sullevan and Scobie Breasley at Haydock Park on the frustrating day in November 1968 when Be Friendly's bid for a third Vernons Sprint Cup was thwarted by fog

'In front of the main stand, two workers were unloading wooden chairs from a tumbril, anchored by a sullen shire horse' – the Hoppegarten in Berlin in March 1990

Finnure and Dick Francis

John Oaksey and Proud Tarquin lead Ron Barry and The Dikler over the last in the 1974 Whitbread

Linwell (Michael Scudamore) returns to the unsaddling enclosure after winning the 1957 Cheltenham Gold Cup. Behind the horse, with the leading rein around his neck, is travelling head lad Jack Smith, and immediately to the left of him is Ivor Herbert. (Immediately right of Michael Scudamore's head is John Lawrence, now John Oaksey)

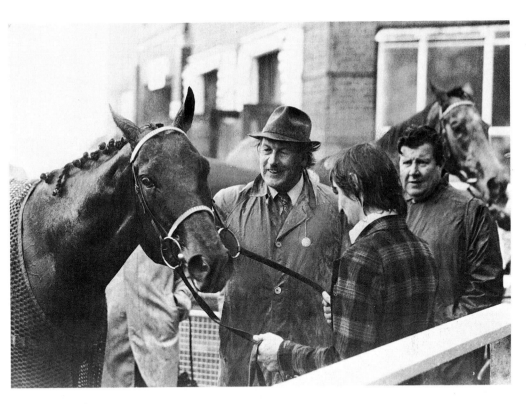

The rewards of ownership. *Above:* Peter Bromley and Treasury Bond at Goodwood. *Below:* Julian Wilson with co-owners Joë Farmer and Norah Hunter-Blair after Tumbledownwind's Gimcrack in 1977. Julian confesses that he still has one of the bottles of Dom Ruinart 'to drink on my death-bed!'

'He was a galloping companion to Mill Reef, and just a little of that brilliance rubbed off': Winter Fair and Clement Freud before the Haydock Park match with Sir Hugh Fraser, September 1972

Trainer Jim 'Duckpond' Old with Superfluous, the horse that never beat another home

The exotic splendour of l'Hippodrome Fandresena d'Ambohimandroso in Madagascar. *Above:* The grandstand. *Below:* Marcus Armytage on Falilalao – 'I think he'd have been better off herding the cattle, which was presumably his full-time job'

Christopher Poole can start visiting car showrooms as Scobie Breasley brings Charlottown back after the 1966 Derby

Matthew Engel
MUCKLE FLUGGA'S LOCAL

On any racecourse map of Britain (as on maps showing major industries, cricket grounds and sun-drenched beaches) there is a large white space when you get near the top. It must be a bit tough being a racing fan way up in the Highlands and Islands. There is no Flat racing north of Edinburgh. Nothing at all happens north of Perth. And in dead of winter they are probably off at Plumpton or Folkestone before the *Life* and *Post* have arrived in Lerwick.

But if there is still a lighthouseman on Muckle Flugga, the absolute dead-end, northernmost tip of the British Isles, and if he happens to be reading this, then I can exclusively reveal to him that he has a racecourse a mere 150 miles away, not south but north-west – out in the stormy North Atlantic at Torshavn in the Faeroe Islands. Torshavn races make even Perth and Edinburgh seem like Ascot.

The Faeroes are sort of Danish, though they are nowhere near Denmark. Their population is under 50,000 and they do not feature largely in world sporting history. But in 1990 they were allowed to compete in the European Soccer Championship for the first time. They were not even allowed to play home matches at home: the pitches were unsuitable. No matter. They began playing Austria (population: rather more than 50,000) in Sweden and won 1–0: the goalkeeper, Jens-Martin Knudsen, and his bobble hat became famous all over Europe. Subsequently, they drew away to Northern Ireland.

I would have gone to see one of their internationals if they were allowed to play them at home but I went instead on St Olaf's Day, 29 July. This is the anniversary of the death, in the year 1030, of the Norse king and saint Olaf Haraldsson and also the Faeroese national holiday: the traditional date for opening parliament,

129

dressing up in ethnic costume, staging a fearsomely contested rowing regatta in the harbour, getting extremely drunk and, in the hills above the capital, going to Torshavn races.

The course comprises a straight track of rolled mud, not quite a mile long and about 10 yards wide. It is not what you would call a track for long-striding gallopers. But it doesn't need to be. The horses are really just a wiry strain of pony, imported from either Norway or – and these are the toughies – from Iceland. The Faeroe islands, where 60 degrees constitutes a heatwave, are no place for any over-delicate animal.

It is all very, very amateur. In view of the problems about lining up the field, the horses race in time trials, usually three at a time. There is no betting (at least, no one admitted that there was any betting). Anyway, the Faeroese have enough problems with their real little weakness. By the afternoon of St Olaf's Day a very large percentage of the population is entirely paralytic. The races here are perhaps unique internationally in attracting only the most sober members of the community: the drunks are still lurching through the streets clutching bottles of beer and vodka. It is generally assumed that Britain has strange licensing laws. Not from this perspective, it doesn't. The bars in the Faeroes were closed down before the First World War and anyone who wants a drink is forced to order it in bulk from Denmark. There is a maximum: a crate of spirits a quarter. So people order a crate a quarter and drink it at once, mostly on St Olaf's Night.

Off Torshavn. Result Torshavn. My friend Andrass the optician was beaten in his heat by Valdemar the ironmonger. The winner was Graekaris the shoemaker on his little chestnut. There was a cup for him but no prize money. Indeed, the custom is for the winner to have open house that night and crack open anything that might be left in his crate. It's tough at the top on Europe's most obscure racecourse.

Matthew Engel is a feature writer and sports columnist on the Guardian. *He is an exceptionally shrewd but incredibly unlucky punter and has lost money on racecourses in five continents.*

Marcus Armytage
THE MOTHER OF NUMBER ONE

Dream the dream: an invitation to ride on a honeymoon isle, south of the equator. No trousers or jumpers needed, nothing but shorts, sun cream, camera. Not to be turned down.

Madagascar. Just over twice the size of Great Britain, it looks like a chip of eastern Africa that's drifted into the Indian Ocean. With a tropical climate, its main business is agriculture, the production of coffee and vanilla for export and rice and cassava for home consumption. Rich in colourful mineral stone, much of it quarried haphazardly, and a haven for wildlife. Mauritius, the Seychelles and Réunion are just a few days' floating on Kon-Tiki away.

Picture it: sitting in the sun, a lemur swinging out of the trees to steal a banana off the table. Paradise could not be too far removed from Madagascar.

For me it had been a great year. It is unlikely that I will ever surpass 1990 in achievement as an amateur rider. In April Mr Frisk had carried me round Aintree in a style even I, a dreamy type, could never have envisaged; and he'd gone on to become the first to complete the Grand National–Whitbread double. I'd ridden in Europe, been to Russia, finished fifth in the famous Pardubice, the world's greatest race after the National and, on leaving for Madagascar, was in an unassailable position in the Fegentri (European amateur riders') championship. An upset, something to restore my size 10s to the ground, was odds-on, but when things are going so well, you begin to forget that they can also go wrong.

The journey to Madagascar was a long one, twelve hours on from Paris. I travelled with Dutch amateur Ronald Van Der Kraats, courtesy of Air France who were to sponsor the two races at l'Hippodrome Fandresena d'Ambohimandroso, a long name for a short course.

Acting as a spare parts courier service, mainly new cylinders, for our host's 20-year-old Peugeot, our luggage was uncarryably heavy. Porters, who outnumbered passengers two to one, scrambled and begged to relieve us of our kit. Being of a suspicious nature, though, I preferred to struggle with my own.

Madagascar, the Democratic Republic of, seems to the casual observer anything but democratic: in a word, corrupt. To get anything important, cash in the right person's pocket never did anyone any harm. It's also the sort of place where, if you repeat a word in grand-sounding tones often enough – spanner or toilet for example – to a native, he'll end up calling his next-born after it. You could put money on there being Spanners and Toilets around.

We were met by our host, Bebe, a small, round fellow who spoke only the native Malagasy and French. The island was once a French colony and French remains a principal language. The only wonder is that it was two missionary Englishmen who helped the Malagasy peoples with their own language, inventing an alphabet. Why they couldn't have taught them some English at the same time heaven knows.

We trooped to the battered Peugeot, its tyres patched and split, its driver's door permanently jammed – but in good shape for a car that had spent twenty years here. We were waiting for the heat to hit us but instead there was a cool breeze. The little car wound its way past mud huts, scruffy inquisitive children, paddy fields and wading washerwomen towards the British Consulate where we picked up a Union Jack for Sunday's racing. Next stop was the Dutch equivalent. How comforting it was to see fellow Europeans who knew the score in this country. We'd only been there an hour and already I was counting the days to the end of the fortnight.

That was Wednesday. The rest of the week was relatively incident-free. Bebe ran an optician's shop in the capital Antananarivo, although I never saw him sell or repair a monocle, let alone a pair of spectacles. It was a monotonous affair, waiting in his shop for closing time so we could get out of the polluted atmosphere of the crowded city at rush hour. Antananarivo made the air of Los Angeles seem as fresh as an Alpine meadow. And to get to bed at nine o'clock every night, electricity in Bebe's house being erratic after dark, was a relief.

Bebe's house, in the 'commuter belt' three miles from the town centre, had an acre of ground and a couple of boxes. His stable lad and jockey was called Eddy, a tall, handsome youth without a job. He was later to be renamed 'Local Hero'.

The days were usually spent wandering round the markets where in the pleasant parts fruit was stacked high in great piles: wild strawberries, green bananas. On the stalls selling dried fish and fresh meat, mainly that of a long-horned cow called a vachu, children were kept in full-time employment swatting flies.

As the big day approached the weather took a turn for the worse. No longer was it raining only at night, it was cloudy all day – and chilly; I was going to get my money's worth from the one precautionary jumper and pair of jeans I'd brought. Rumours about the place, specifically, about the track, grew. Yves Saint-Martin rode here on his world retirement tour and was so concerned about it that he pulled up after a furlong. Terrified of pickpockets, I walked around with my hand constantly attached to my wallet and anything else readily detachable from myself.

The big day began brightly enough. It was to be the high point of the stay. And what was more, my girlfriend Mouse was due to arrive.

The trip to l'Hippodrome Fandresena d'Ambohimandroso is counted not in hours or miles but rather in punctures. One stoppage between two cars is considered good going, verging on the miraculous. The year before, they had stopped four times for punctures. Having seen the splits in our tyres before we set off, it was with some consternation on my part that Eddy screamed round corners, scattering chickens and children in our wake. And, when we did come to a halt on an open piece of road – as we occasionally did waiting for the second little car to catch up – we would be surrounded by peasants selling toys and strawberries, apparently miles from nowhere.

We pressed on urgently throughout an electrical storm until, after three hours, we came to a track off the main road. It was blocked by a pig which two villagers were trying vainly to drive in the right direction with sticks. Half a mile of rough track and we had arrived – in the middle of the scrub. Long grass and small bushes; a herd of vachu grazing, unconcerned that they were stripping the home turn of l'Hippodrome of any remaining vegetation.

A vaguely oval circuit was marked out, 1,000 yards round, firm and flat. A small thatched stand stood opposite the winning post. There was no one there. A minibus was to be our changing room and the scales, a swinging basket attached to the tree, were to weigh us all, regardless of height, size or actual weight, at approximately nine stone. How flattering. I had not been that weight since I was about 14.

Locals arrived in dribs and drabs with the rain. Cold? It was freezing. The crowd was dressed 'informally' – stroll on Ascot with your dress regulations. One man looked very fetching in his woollen dressing gown; some children wore nothing. Some wore shorts, there were various shirts, skirts and track suits, and most females, regardless of age, carried children on their backs, tied on with a shawl. The only common features among the *haute couture* of Fandresena were that none of it was clean and most wore straw hats.

When it began to rain, the crowd improvised mackintoshes from plastic sacks. Local jockeys appeared, like the crowd, from nowhere; a keen one, in colours similar to those of the Aga Khan, had his glass pilot's goggles pulled down before weighing out. Helmets were secured with string, whips were all shapes and sizes. And it rained.

We walked the course not knowing whether to laugh or cry. The stalls were a permanent fixture, knarled knotty branches nailed together. The bends were tight, the going firm despite the rain and the vachu seemed disinclined to move. And it rained.

The next major shock was the 'horses'. I weighed out with bridle, saddle and girths. A fellow whom I assumed to be my trainer, called Raharijaona, collected the bridle and set off for the bush. Another dragged me along five minutes later with the saddle, and the search for my mount began. And a complicated affair it was too. About twenty-five pot-bellied ponies were tied up to various larger bushes, grazing. There was not a muscle between them and they ranged in height from about thirteen to about fifteen hands. We moved from bush to bush, pony to pony. I had no idea how I would spot my mount and to make matters worse I was being followed by an ever-growing crowd of inquisitive, giggling children. At about the tenth pony I recognized the green reins of my bridle attached to a chestnut, surrounded by another posse of village children. There were knots in the cheek-straps of the bridle and still the bit was hanging out of his mouth, along with a sprig of the bush itself. This was my mount Falilalao. How do you do?

Falilalao walked out of the makeshift stalls and never saw which way the others went. A short choppy-striding animal, I think he'd have been better off herding the cattle, which was presumably his full-time job. I failed to get him out of a canter. However, that was nothing; Van Der Kraats – now there's a horseman – was lapped on his grey, Irinavola, who had used up all his energy in one buck, before pulling up.

And it rained, verging on a tropical storm. The British Consul had turned up in his Range Rover (only the Consuls had decent vehicles in Madagascar), the most waterproof shelter within a fifty-mile radius and, much to my relief, Mouse had turned up with a handful of other Brits.

The locals had run another race while we prepared for our second rides, Van Der Kraats on Imperiale, myself on Tollichka, a mare. The rain had now necessitated a move from the bush to a thatched yard where all the boxes had been taken over by 'racegoers'. Consequently our horses were saddled in the rain. I would have commented at this stage that saddling outside the boxes seemed to defeat their purpose, but I was far beyond cynicism by now.

In the paddock two things struck me. First, a purposeful but clearly unshy local dressed in rags, presumably on his way from one 'parish' to another, decided that he needed a pee. Nothing wrong in that. Well, the urge coincided with the time he crossed the paddock, it being directly on his route. So, in front of an admiring audience of several hundred who never once flinched or gave him a second look, our purposeful friend took out the necessary equipment and, without stopping, peed his way across the paddock. What is more, he didn't have any shoes on!

It was quite obvious to Van Der Kraats and myself that Eddy was the local hero: as Lester is to Epsom, so Eddy was to the course with the long name. All the horses with one exception were in this apology of a paddock. Practising a few imaginary square cuts with my whip as we waited, I attracted the attention of the only other European apart from our party and the Consul. 'You must be English,' he said, flattering my square cut. As he said it, the first proper horse we had seen was paraded into the paddock to rapturous applause from the crowd. Not only did it look like Mill

135

Reef, it had plainly had a square meal recently (something that couldn't be said for Tollichka), it sported a smart rug and a sheepskin noseband, it was three hands higher than my pony and it was about to be mounted by Local Hero.

'We might as well go home,' I commented to my companion. 'You might as well,' he agreed, nodding at 'Mill Reef'. And, withdrawing his racecard from the shelter of his jacket pocket, he pointed to the breeding of Tollichka and Imperiale and added: 'You might as well, because yours is also the mother of number one!'

P.S. Some of the names have been changed to protect innocent horses.

I would like to thank the British and Dutch Consuls for making our stay, which we expensively cut short by a week, more bearable.

'Mill Reef' won unopposed and Mouse spent the next week in Addenbrookes Hospital, Cambridge, suffering from an unidentified tropical illness.

Marcus Armytage ekes out a living as a freelance writer working mainly for the Racing Post, Field, Horse & Hound *and* Daily Telegraph. *He spends that living satisfying his desire to race, preferably at speed, over obstacles on an unpaid basis. He has met with some degree of success in this department, notably with Mr Frisk.*

Days at the races

Joe Hirsch
WITNESSES TO PERFECTION

On the morning of 9 June 1973, anticipation was thick as porridge all across the United States. It had been twenty-five years since the last Triple Crown winner – Citation in 1948 – and an entire generation of racing fans had grown to maturity wondering if they would ever see another.

But this was the Year of The Red Horse, and there was hope. The Red Horse was Secretariat, a huge, muscular red chestnut colt by Bold Ruler out of Somethingroyal by Princequillo, owned by the Meadow Stable, trained by Lucien Laurin, and ridden by Ron Turcotte. An outstanding two-year-old champion with seven victories from nine starts, he was hailed as a special horse from the outset. His sire was immensely successful, both as a racehorse and as a stallion, and if his stamina was suspect, his brilliance was not. The dam had produced several top horses for the Chenery family, owners of Meadow Stud, and she, too, enjoyed a sparkling reputation. So even before he raced at three, Secretariat was a household name. And then, at the turn of the year, owner-breeder Christopher T. Chenery, who had been ill for several years, died, leaving a sizeable estate. Millions of dollars were needed to pay the taxes on the estate, and the syndication of Secretariat was the only solution.

Two players stepped forward for important roles in the ensuing drama. One was Helen Chenery Tweedy, daughter of C. T. Chenery. Of the three Chenery children, she was the only one with an abiding interest in racing and she was determined to continue the family participation in the sport. The other was 23-year-old Seth Hancock, who took over as head of Claiborne Farm in the autumn of 1972 following the death of his Father, Bull Hancock, of cancer. Bull Hancock was probably the most influential man in American racing at the time of his death, and it was he who arranged for the Chenerys' mare, Somethingroyal, to go to Bold Ruler, owned by the Phipps family, on a two-time basis, with one foal to go to the Phippses and the other to go to the Chenerys. Secretariat went to the Chenerys on the flip of a coin.

Seth Hancock and Helen Chenery Tweedy agreed on terms for the syndication of Secretariat in February 1973. The colt would be offered at an unbelievable $190,000 a share for thirty-two shares, or a total of just over $6 million. Though the price was almost twice as high as the top of the market at the time, it was subscribed in a matter of days, principally by telephone.

Meanwhile, Secretariat himself was in Florida, training for his three-year-old debut under Lucien Laurin, who was trainer by happenstance. His son, Roger Laurin, had been training for the Meadow Stable in 1971 when the Phippses' trainer, Eddie Neloy, died suddenly of a massive heart attack one morning at Belmont Park. The Phippses invited Roger Laurin to train their horses, and young Laurin recommended his father as his successor at Meadow Stable.

After training brilliantly for Lucien Laurin, a peppery little French Canadian who continued to operate a public stable even after taking on the Meadow Stable horses, Secretariat made his first two starts as a three-year-old and won the seven-furlong Bay Shore and Gotham Mile very easily at New York's Aqueduct race track. Thus he was a short-priced favourite when he ran in the Wood Memorial, a major Kentucky Derby prep race, in New York on 21 April, coupled in the wagering with another of Lucien Laurin's horses, Angle Light, owned by Edwin Whittaker. But Secretariat only finished third, behind Angle Light and Sham, and the racing world was stunned. So was Laurin, who forgot he trained the winner and was late in reaching the winner's circle for post-race ceremonies. Everyone in America had his own analysis of the loss. Some felt Bold Rulers were short of stamina. Some felt Secretariat sulked when taken under restraint by Turcotte. Some felt Secretariat was over-rated. Some felt an abscess on the colt's gum prevented him from grabbing the bit as he normally did. Those who paid $190,000 for a share were concerned, with the Kentucky Derby only a fortnight away. Indeed, the furore continued un-abated up to Derby Day. On the day before the Derby, a radio commentator announced that Secretariat had broken down. Lucien Laurin, who had left the colt in perfect condition at Churchill Downs an hour earlier, rushed to the track – to find Secretariat resting easily in his box.

But all the fuss ended in the twilight of 5 May when Secretariat, starting from post position 10, came from far back in a field of thirteen to win the Run for the Roses by more than two lengths in the record time of 1:59 2/5, a mark that still stands. Sham was second and Our Native finished third; Forego was fourth. Two weeks later, at Pimlico racecourse in Baltimore, Secretariat, Laurin and Turcotte had a surprise in store for everyone. Secretariat came out of the gate last in a field of six, but after a furlong and a half accelerated dramatically and went from last to first in a twinkling. The huge crowd gasped and then sat back to watch the 3–10 favourite gallop home to win by more than two lengths. *Daily Racing Form* clockers timed The Red Horse in a record 1:53 2/5 for the nine-and-a-half furlongs but the official clocker, who had additional duties that afternoon and was distracted, caught Secretariat in 1:54 2/5 and that became the official time. The Maryland Racing Commission held an enquiry into the timing of the race without reaching any substantive conclusion.

Such was the background as Secretariat prepared to bid for the Triple Crown in the twelve-furlong Belmont Stakes at Belmont Park on 9 June 1973. A crowd of over 67,000 looked on in delightful weather as a field of five went to the post, with Secretariat the 1–10 favourite. Sham, second in the Kentucky Derby and second in the Preakness, was second choice in the Belmont at 5–1.

Secretariat and Sham duelled for the lead from the outset and stayed together for six furlongs. At this point Sham began to drop back and Secretariat continued on steadily. After eight furlongs The Red Horse was seven lengths in front and the issue was no longer in doubt. Two furlongs out Secretariat was leading by twenty lengths and now the crowd got into it. As Secretariat turned into the two-furlong straight, men, women and children, caught up in a frenzy of admiration, stood on their seats and waved furiously or jumped up and down on the ground, pounding their fists in the air and shouting for Secretariat. The noise washed down from the huge stands like a tidal wave and seemed to galvanize the horse. He continued to streak away from distant pursuers, led by twenty-eight lengths with a furlong remaining and galloped on strongly to win by thirty-one lengths.

The applause and the cheering were deafening, and when it was announced that Secretariat had set a track record of 2:24 for the mile-and-a-half – against the old mark of 2:26 3/5 – the noise was beyond belief. People laughed, shouted, cried, roared to the limit of their physical strength, and yet when The Red Horse returned to the unsaddling enclosure, the sound level increased still further. It was a hysterical reception on the greatest day of racing America had known. People were aware that for the first time in their lives – and probably the last – they had witnessed perfection.

Joe Hirsch is executive columnist of the Daily Racing Form *in the USA.*

Christopher Poole
CHARLOTTOWN'S DERBY

George Windlass literally had a hand in winning the 1966 Derby; but you will find no mention of his name among the records of Charlottown's triumph that day at Epsom. George was a calm man with steady habits and powerful hands, an artisan of the old school. He was on Epsom Downs a quarter-century ago by special request and the foresight displayed by Gordon Smyth, Charlottown's trainer, in inviting him to attend the Derby paid a remarkable dividend.

George was the Lewes blacksmith. All the trainers in the then flourishing racing centre in and around the county town of Sussex called on his services and he would make his languid journey from one yard to another on an elderly bicycle. Lewes is a hilly town and George pushed as often as he rode. He was certainly not given to rushing and that characteristic was to play a vital role in Charlottown's victory in the premier Classic.

George Windlass had experienced trouble with shoeing Charlottown from the horse's juvenile days when Towser Gosden, father of present-day Newmarket trainer John, handled Lady Zia Wernher's bay colt. But George, he of the steady habits and steady hands, always managed to secure racing plates to those shelly feet with a little extra effort and a little muttering. Trainer Smyth, who had taken over the Gosden string – Charlottown included – at the conclusion of the 1965 season when ill health forced Towser into retirement, decided George had better travel to Epsom with his Derby hope. Just in case . . .

Derby Day in 1966 was wet enough to send for Noah, the rain becoming heavier as the big-race runners went on parade. Michael Jarvis, now a Prix de l'Arc de Triomphe winning trainer, led up Charlottown, the mount of Australian ace Scobie Breasley. Any

143

Derby parade is tense enough; this one, with rain slanting across the Downs, was especially so. And it was at that moment that Charlottown lost his near-fore shoe.

George was sent for. He didn't rush. The others would just have to wait while he re-plated the heavily backed colt. Methodically he set about the task, muttering a little but calm as ever. It took the thick end of fifteen minutes for George fully to satisfy himself that Charlottown was ready to face the race of his life.

'He did such a good job that the shoe stayed in place for a fortnight,' recalls Gordon Smyth. 'Charlottown would never have won his Derby without the skills of George Windlass. In the circumstances, he displayed the most remarkable professionalism.'

So did Scobie Breasley. He had come in for the Epsom ride only after fellow Australian Ron Hutchinson had given an uncharacteristic and inept display on the colt in the Lingfield Trial and been sacked by the owner. Breasley, although he had won two years earlier on Ireland's Santa Claus, had been without a mount. The late booking allowed him only two canters with Charlottown on the Lewes gallops, little enough by way of getting-to-know-you sessions. Yet he was to give the Wernher three-year-old a perfect ride.

But then Lady Zia and her husband, Major General Sir Harold Wernher, had always been lucky owners. Their own story is a romantic one. Lady Zia was the daughter of Grand Duke Michael of Russia and the Countess de Torby. Russian born, she married Sir Harold in 1917 and so escaped the revolution. Cecil Boyd-Rochfort was her first trainer and it was he who, for just 600 guineas, bought Double Life who won the Chesterfield Cup and Cesarewitch for Lady Zia before becoming the foundation mare of her Someries Stud at Newmarket. Double Life bred Precipitation, winner of an Ascot Gold Cup and sire of 1946 Derby scorer Airborne. Persian Gulf was another son of Double Life. He won a wartime Coronation Cup (1944) and sired Parthia whom Boyd-Rochfort trained to land the 1959 Derby in the colours of Sir Humphrey de Trafford. But the family of Double Life is best remembered for producing that great racemare Meld, heroine of the fillies' Triple Crown in 1955 and the dam of Charlottown.

Sir Harold Wernher's good fortune as an owner came close to that of his wife. Keenly interested in steeplechasing – he was at one time Master of the Fernie – Sir Harold bought Brown Jack to go jumping. That outstanding stayer won the Champion Hurdle of 1928 but it was on the Flat that he was to become so greatly loved. Partnered by Steve Donoghue, the Irish-bred gelding won Royal Ascot's Queen Alexandra Stakes for six successive seasons. That wonderful achievement, together with victories in the Chester, Doncaster and Goodwood Cups and the Ebor Handicap, earned Brown Jack folk hero status much like that enjoyed by Desert Orchid today.

In all, Brown Jack won seven times over hurdles and eighteen races on the Flat to earn nearly £30,000, a huge figure for a gelding in his era. Sir Harold had given just £750 for him to the Irish trainer and dealer Charles Rogers in 1927 – a contingency of £50 being added to the deal if the horse ever won a race! Brown Jack lived on in retirement at his owner's home until 1948 and no horse could ever replace him in Sir Harold's affections. But there was another high-class animal to carry Harold Wernher's colours and this one forged the link between the aristocratic owning family and Towser Gosden's Lewes stable which was to lead to Charlottown's Derby. That horse was Aggressor, home-bred at the Someries Stud and foaled in 1955. There is quite a story behind the son of Combat being sent to Gosden.

In the summer of 1956, Sir Harold and Cecil Boyd-Rochfort went to the Blackhall Stud near the Curragh, where all the Someries foals were brought on after weaning, to look over that year's crop. Both Wernher and his trainer were disappointed with the appearance of Aggressor and considered him well below standard. It was decided to sell the plain-looking youngster at the Ballsbridge Yearling Sales the following September, and up he went to Dublin with a reserve of just £1,000. Ballsbridge bidders were not keen on him either and the top offer was only 750 guineas. Boyd-Rochfort did not want the colt so Sir Harold picked Gosden, a man with a well-earned reputation as a brilliant handicap specialist, to handle Aggressor, for whom no Classic entries had been made.

Aggressor, at his best on soft ground, was to enjoy a fine career under Gosden's care. In all he won eleven races worth £36,203, which sounds a modest sum in today's terms but was worth a great deal more over thirty years ago. He reached his peak as a five-year-old, landing Newbury's John Porter Stakes, the Hardwicke Stakes at Royal Ascot and, as a wonderful testament to Towser Gosden's abilities, the 1960 King George VI and Queen Elizabeth Stakes, in which he beat the great filly Petite Etoile under a typically elegant ride from Jimmy Lindley. Clearly well pleased with all this, Sir Harold and Lady Zia had a horse or two with Gosden most subsequent seasons and finally decided to send Meld's son by the Prix du Jockey-Club and Grand Prix de Paris winner Charlottesville to Lewes.

John Montague Gosden, a farmer's son from near the Sussex seaside resort of Eastbourne, first held a training licence in 1928 when in his early twenties. But it was after the Second World War, when he moved to Heath House at Lewes, that this master of his craft (always known as Towser) began to establish a reputation for excellence in his stables. Had he been able to find high-quality horses earlier in his career, Gosden might well have produced a handful of Classic winners. As it was, he 'farmed' the big handicaps, winning the Manchester November, then a mighty betting race, no fewer than four times. Gosden's health was never robust. He joined the RAF on the outbreak of war but was invalided out and came home to combine farming with training a few horses until the end of hostilities. Finally, the racing fates were to prove unkind to him. Gosden was a dying man when the 1965 Flat racing season reached its conclusion and, despite his high hopes for Charlottown's Derby challenge the following summer, felt he was unable to continue training. Heath House, the horses and those hopes passed to Gordon Smyth, who moved across Sussex from Arundel, handing over at the Castle Stables there to his assistant, John Dunlop. But at least Towser Gosden lived long enough to know that 'his' colt had won the Derby.

Sir Harold and Lady Zia Wernher were seriously rich. He had been chairman of the huge Electrolux Corporation, she had brought from Russia a fabled collection of precious objects including the largest collection of Fabergé jewelled eggs in private hands. They were not, however, known for open-handed presents. Scobie Breasley, for example, had his Derby percentage topped up with the gift of a gravy boat – silver-plated! He laughs about it to this day. I have no idea if George Windlass received a thank-you handout of any kind – but I did very well out of Charlottown's narrow Epsom success in the rain-soaked Derby of 1966.

My old car was on its last legs and, much encouraged by the Lewes fish-and-chip shop owner Cyril Sheppard who had battered his way to a small fortune and had a horse in the yard, I backed Charlottown with every spare quid ante-post throughout the winter of 1965–6. Thanks to the calm knowledge of George Windlass and the race-riding brilliance of Scobie Breasley, I arrived at Royal Ascot a couple of weeks later in a shining new motor.

Charlottown might not have been one of the great Derby winners but he has always been a firm favourite with me.

Christopher Poole has been racing correspondent of the London Evening Standard *since 1970 and has made more than 2000 radio broadcasts for BBC World Service. He has also written or edited 14 books devoted to racing.*

Peter Scott
FORTY-SIX DERBYS, ONLY ONE EPSOM

Edward Tudor, now generally and deservedly forgotten by Turf historians, carried my money in the first of forty-six Derbys I have been fortunate to see. His cowardly display at least did me the favour of helping to establish early on that I was not clever enough to beat the bookmakers.

Edward Tudor's sire, Hyperion, and full brother, Owen Tudor, were both Derby winners. His own obvious talent made Edward Tudor one of those horses for whom excuses are continually produced – not fully fit, distance too short or too long, met with interference at a crucial stage, etc. The 1946 Flat season opened with forecasts that the 'five Hyperions' – Gulf Stream, Khaled, Radiotherapy and Aldis Lamp were the others – would dominate the colts' Classics. This did not happen, although Gulf Stream, Khaled and Radiotherapy were placed in the Two Thousand Guineas or Derby.

Epsom drew an enormous crowd for the first post-war Derby. I took up a rails position facing Tattenham Corner and had an excellent view as the runners swept round. Edward Tudor was lobbing along in third place with nearly all his opponents off the bit.

'Gordon has done it at last,' shouted my neighbour, but there was no loudspeaker commentary in those days and we could not see the finish. News percolated through that Airborne, at 50–1, had made a powerful late run to beat Gulf Stream. Edward Tudor finished sixth and race reports made it clear that he had thrown in the towel under pressure. Gordon Richards had to wait another seven years to score a Derby win at what turned out to be his final attempt. From boyhood I had idolized Gordon, and Pinza's Coronation week triumph, following closely on a well deserved knighthood, remains my greatest racing thrill.

148

Gordon also played a part in the Derby's 200th running, won in 1979 by Troy from one of the race's strongest post-war fields. Troy scored by seven lengths in the colours of Sir Michael Sobell, whom Gordon had in 1960 advised to buy the Ballymacoll Stud from Miss Dorothy Paget's executors. Sir Michael had already tasted beginner's luck. London Cry, his first horse, was trained by Gordon to win the 1958 Cambridgeshire. The purchase of Ballymacoll moved Sir Michael into the big league, and among the mares to change hands in that deal was Troy's granddam, Pin Prick.

Gordon trained the Sobell horses until his retirement in 1970, when he became Sir Michael's racing manager with trainer Major Dick Hern. I doubt if any post-war Derby winner has finished faster than did Troy, who preceded Henbit and Nashwan in the first of three triumphs for Hern and Willie Carson. Nashwan, far superior to his 1989 opponents, gave Willie few Epsom problems, but on Troy Carson had to sit and suffer, waiting for the right time to move. Henbit set his jockey the task of getting home first on a horse who had cracked his off-fore cannon bone in the final furlong. This tragic injury meant that 1980's celebrations were muted in comparison with those for Troy and the cheers which greeted Hern when wheeling his chair into the winner's enclosure to greet Nashwan.

Carson also excelled on Hot Grove in 1977, but he was beaten a neck. Finishing second in the Derby has been likened to losing an FA Cup semi-final: so near and yet so far from the mecca of Wembley. Willie's enterprise on Hot Grove early in the straight poached what looked a decisive lead and it required all Lester Piggott's strength to force The Minstrel in front close home. First and second finished five lengths clear of third placed Blushing Groom, but one national newspaper writer reported that Derby battle without even mentioning Hot Grove's name!

Piggott's record of nine Derby wins is unlikely to be beaten – except perhaps by himself. Nijinsky, Teenoso, St Paddy and Empery were among Piggott's fairly straightforward successes, but Roberto (1972) might well have been beaten with any of Lester's contemporaries in the saddle; and his icy late swoop on Sir Ivor used that colt's brilliant finishing speed to spectacular effect and showed how nonchalant Lester can be even on the biggest occasions. Crepello, another of Piggott's winners, cannot have been easy to keep balanced at Epsom. Crepello's 1957 success coincided with Vincent O'Brien's first impact on the Derby. Ballymoss had promising form but was allowed to start at 33–1. Many then thought of his trainer more in terms of Cheltenham or Aintree.

'I expect Ballymoss to run really well,' Vincent told me in his quiet way beforehand. So he did, finishing one and a half lengths behind Crepello in second place. Ballymoss went on to win the St Leger that autumn and his four-year-old campaign included victories in the Coronation Cup, Eclipse Stakes, King George VI and Queen Elizabeth Stakes and Prix de l'Arc de Triomphe. Ballymoss and another of O'Brien's Derby seconds, El Gran Senor, were far superior to Larkspur, the least distinguished of this trainer's six Derby winners. Larkspur's year, 1962, was marred by seven fallers who included the favourite Hethersett.

Sea Bird was given rave reviews after his 1965 win, but Mill Reef, who also landed the Arc in the same year as his Derby triumph, was to my mind a better and more versatile horse. Sea Bird did not win the Arc by anything like the official margin of six lengths but that is another story. The 1970s was a vintage decade for Derby winners, Mill Reef following Nijinsky with Grundy and Troy to come. All carried off a string of big races. Pat Eddery rode Grundy besides Golden Fleece and Quest For Fame, whose overall records were nothing like so good. Time has not been kind to Grundy's reputation, whereas I believe that Shergar, like Sea Bird, did not fully deserve all the superlatives heaped on him. Shergar could not have done more than win in the style he did, but Glint of Gold and Kalaglow, his only serious rivals, ruined their chances with an early bumping match. Glint of Gold made up many lengths to be second, while Kalaglow was so badly hurt that he could not run again until the following season; then he proved himself a real star. Shergar, meanwhile, bowed out with a dismal St Leger display for which no satisfactory explanation was ever given. His abduction and almost certain death early in his stud career gave him added 'romance', but his only crop to race did not particularly impress and I doubt whether he would have been a stallion success.

Shahrastani and Kahyasi followed Shergar as Derby winners for the Aga Khan. Shahrastani was fortunate to beat Dancing Brave at Epsom but had become a really good horse on Irish Derby day. Sadly, this peak was short-lived. He 'boiled over' on King George afternoon whereas Dancing Brave went from strength to strength. Dancing Brave was among the few genuinely unfortunate Derby losers I have seen. Riding tactics, rather than the course, were to blame; but anyone can be wise with hindsight, and Greville Starkey was trying to relax a colt whose stamina had been suspect beforehand. Starkey's greatest season was eight years earlier in 1978 when he won a photo-finish Derby on Shirley Heights.

Arthur Budgett rated Morston superior to Blakeney of the two Derby winners he owned, trained and bred, but Blakeney had tremendous courage and did well at stud. He tackled the Ascot Gold Cup as a four-year-old, when firm ground contributed to his defeat by Precipice Wood. Blakeney came back to middle-distance racing a month later and finished a good second to Nijinsky in the King George.

Charlie Smirke was in the Piggott class as a big race rider. Their 1952 Derby duel on Tulyar and Gay Time provided a memorable clash between veteran and teenager. Smirke won again on Hard Ridden six years later and emerged from the weighing room to announce he would soon retire. 'That was the grand finale, chaps,' he told waiting pressmen.

Australian riders to win the Derby during the post-war years have included Pat Glennon (Sea Bird), Neville Sellwood (Larkspur) and George Moore, whose success on Royal Palace provided one of three victories for Sir Noel Murless's stable. Australians to have made a still bigger mark on the race were Rae Johnstone and Scobie Breasley. Rae excelled on Galcador, when beating Prince Simon, and again on the unsound Lavandin. Scobie followed Santa Claus (1964) with a brilliant ride on Charlottown two years later.

Steve Cauthen, like Steve Donoghue, has not been afraid to use forcing tactics in the Derby, leading throughout on both Reference Point and Slip Anchor. Reference Point had the better overall record. Slip Anchor was spectacular on Derby day, but Cauthen's enterprise played a part in his seven-length margin as it did with Old Vic in the 1989 Prix du Jockey-Club.

Psidium and Phil Drake won the Derby from what looked hopeless positions at Tattenham Corner. Psidium's year was notable for the lead changing hands eight times in the straight, but 1949 provided the closest post-war Derby battle, with Nimbus beating Amour Drake and Swallow Tail in a three-way photo. Phil

Drake, ridden by Freddy Palmer, emulated Rae Johnstone's first Derby winner, My Love, in going on to take the Grand Prix de Paris. Phil Drake's time at Longchamp set a new world grass course record for 3,000 metres. Security was not so strict in Phil Drake's day: I remember him standing a few hours later in an unattended horsebox, waiting to leave Epsom. I was able to climb up and give the 1955 Derby winner a 'well done' pat.

The Grand Prix de Paris lost all its old character when shortened to ten furlongs in 1987. At least one leading French owner-breeder felt that the changed distance should go with a new title, but a move to re-name it the Grand Prix de Longchamp was blocked by the municipal authorities. Until after the Second World War, the Prix du Jockey-Club was confined to French-breds, but it has now long superseded the Grand Prix de Paris as France's premier three-year-old race.

The Irish Derby was far later than the Prix du Jockey-Club in emerging as a major international test. Its 36lb weights range once gave this event the appearance of a handicap. Its present title was assumed in 1866 after short-lived predecessors the O'Derby Stakes and The Curragh Derby. Not until 1962 did it assume major importance. Since then ten Epsom winners have gone on to success in Ireland, the latest being Generous.

Despite overseas competitors, there remains one pre-eminent Derby, run over a course with hills and camber demanding balance and courage besides class. If I were allowed to watch only one race a year, it would always be the Derby – at Epsom.

Peter Scott, a racing writer since 1950, was 'Hotspur' on the Daily Telegraph *for 26 years until 1991. Now a freelance, he is also on the Board of United Racecourses Ltd, which controls Epsom, Sandown Park and Kempton Park.*

Julian Wilson
GOOD GOING

It began at around 4.00 a.m. and continued at a soft persistent monotone.

The rain.

They had said that it would rain but that had merely made the waiting worse.

It was Thursday 18 August 1977, the morning of the 132nd running of the Gimcrack Stakes. The favourite was Tumbledownwind, owned in partnership by a broadcaster (half share) and two delightful ladies (quarter shares), for one of whom this was a fortuitous first experience of ownership.

Tumbledownwind did not like soft going. It is a fact that rain is liable to make the going soft.

The broadcaster lay awake, tossing from side to side, in Room 523 of the Viking Hotel. It was a long, long vigil from 4.00 a.m. till the time that the newspapers were delivered at 7.00 a.m. For the hundredth time he thought back over the barely believable events of the preceding 10 months.

Yes, of course he wanted to buy a yearling! Why did the trainer bother to ask? But this time let's try to buy a middle-distance horse. In the broadcaster's view the fashion for speed and precocity was making it easier to win three-year-old races of a mile and a half upwards. So let's buy a horse with a mile and a half pedigree. The broadcaster had promised his wife a few days in Paris in October 1976, so three yearlings were marked off in the October Sales catalogue: colts by Sun Prince (1¼m), Morston (1½m) and Tumble Wind (1½m).

'Buy the one you like most – but don't go beyond 5,000 guineas,' was the order.

And so began the saga of Tumbledownwind, for the successful

153

purchase was the bay colt by Tumble Wind (USA) out of Miss Pinkerton, by Above Suspicion. Price 4,800 guineas.

The course of events in horse racing is rarely smooth. Within two weeks of the purchase of the Tumble Wind colt, two substantial accounts arrived on the broadcaster's desk: (1) for the afore-mentioned animal and (2) from a voracious bookmaker demanding settlement of a series of ante-post wagers (losing variety) on a filly named Welsh Flame in the 1976 Cambridgeshire. It did not require a degree in advanced mathematics for the recipient of these bills to be aware that (1) and (2) equalled substantially more than the figure displayed in the 'Credit' column of a recently received bank statement. It was thus that the partnership was formed between the broadcaster and two charming ladies in Joë Farmer and Norah Hunter-Blair. What was forfeited financially was more than compensated for by long and lasting friendships. (The owner of Welsh Flame, Miss Pat O'Kelly, was more financially fortunate. Welsh Flame has bred five winners to date, and her 1990 yearling filly realized 840,000 guineas. Her grand-daughter is a filly called Salsabil.)

And so began a magical mystery tour, as unreal and unbelievable as it was unexpected. The 'potential stayer' turned out to be the trainer's most precocious two-year-old, and the stable's first two-year-old runner, in April. He was beaten that day, but only by one, at the Newmarket Craven Meeting. At the Guineas Meeting he won by six lengths. He won again at Haydock, and was a beaten favourite at Royal Ascot – second to Sookera.

Was it the end of the beginning, or the beginning of the end?

The broadcaster had a passion for Goodwood. A rented cottage by the sea at West Wittering . . . bucket and spade for the three-year-old son and heir . . . a dream to have a fancied runner. So Tumbledownwind was dispatched to the Sussex coast for the Rous Memorial Stakes.

'I haven't done much with him since Ascot,' said the trainer. 'He'll probably blow up, you know.'

Tumbledownwind won by four lengths, bouncing off the firm ground in course record time. The trainer and stable jockey, televiewing from Newmarket races, could barely believe their eyes.

'What about the Gimcrack?' suggested the broadcaster.

'I don't know about that,' said the trainer. 'I think I'll run Royal Harmony – he's better than yours.'

'Well, run them both,' said the broadcaster.

. . . All that had been two weeks and five days earlier. Fate, as so often happens, had ruled out Royal Harmony, with a minor mishap. Now Tumbledownwind had just four opponents – and the weather – to confront.

Breakfast, at the Viking Hotel, was taken with John de Moraville, correspondent of the *Daily Express*.

'You're not eating a lot,' he ventured.

'It's raining . . .'

'You don't look too good. . . ?'

'I woke up at 4.00 a.m.'

And so the day dragged wearily on, with the feeling that an unseen hand was clutching the root of the abdomen, and gently twisting.

Suitcase packed, and taxi to the races at 11.15; final preparations for the BBC radio commentary (in those days Peter Bromley took his holiday in August); and a polite refusal to an offer to be interviewed on ITV. And still it was raining. The minutes ticked away languidly. The Clerk of the Course obstinately declined to alter the going from 'good'. The first race, over one and a half miles was run in 2 minutes 36.31 seconds – 7.31 seconds slower than standard time. 'Good. . . ?'

Now began the balancing act. The radio commentary position was at least four minutes' walk-and-climb from the paddock.

'Get him saddled and in the paddock early,' the broadcaster nagged the trainer. 'I want to see him!' The ladies, bedecked with splendid, if dampened, millinery, were delightfully a-twitter.

And still it rained.

The John Dunn Show, on Radio 2, joined the action at York around 2.57.

The broadcaster went into auto-pilot. The runners . . . riders . . . draw . . . the going (officially 'good', but . . .), ending with epithets like '. . . confidence greatly diminished . . .'

At last they were 'off'.

'And Tumbledownwind was quickly away from stall one . . .'

The next 1 minute 17.37 seconds were filled with hope, anticipation, concern, despair, reassurance, and ultimately joyous triumph. Very little of the commentary remains in the memory, except a closing line: 'So Tumbledownwind has won the Gimcrack, worth £26,178 to the winner . . . as I return you to London.'

Headphones off . . . an attempt to make a dignified exit from the commentary box . . . and suddenly an overwhelming surge of elation.

There was only one brief moment of disappointment: the long, precipitous, frequently obstructed descent from the roof meant missing by moments the chance to meet the leg-weary hero, who had battled so bravely through the Knavesmire. But then came the glorious presentations, of oceans of delectable Dom Ruinart Blanc de Blancs 1969, and an invitation to a glass of champagne with the Stewards and Race Committee.

'Go on, drink up!' said the trainer.

'But I'm commentating on the Nunthorpe in five minutes' time. I'll have trouble with my words!'

Happily, the Nunthorpe passed without incident (if you can describe four horses within three parts of a length as 'without incident'), the end-of-meeting summary was duly recorded and the package transmitted to London. Now the next decision – to share a case of champagne with colleagues in the press room, or return to London with the jockey on the 5.17 train? In the event option two was chosen and Geoff Lewis and the broadcaster chatted and cat-napped from York to King's Cross.

'You want to sell him, you know. He was flat to the boards today and it wasn't that great a race,' said Geoff.

'Yes, but the ground didn't suit him, did it? And he's as brave as a lion. And I'll never have another one like him . . .'

'Suit yourself,' shrugged Geoff. 'But Ron Smyth thinks you should sell him.'

(It has never become apparent why Ron Smyth, the excellent and experienced Epsom trainer, should have become involved in this discussion, but he did!)

As the train pulled into King's Cross station at 8.00 the game plan became clear.

'Let's have dinner at Pontevecchio,' said the broadcaster. 'My treat.'

Perfectly roasted grouse was washed down by Brunello di Montalcino and Geoff received wave after wave of deserved congratulations, including by phone from his regular golf partner Ronnie Corbett.

At home, in bed, the day went round and round. There were so

many people to thank. The trainer, Bruce Hobbs . . . but he had
thanked the owners! The lad, Tommy Westhead, who had inherited
the horse when his previous attendant had vanished without trace
back to his native Liverpool. The breeder, Eleanor Samuelson,
whom the broadcaster had originally met through a mutual friend,
Liz Burke. The 'ladies', one or both of whom had brought such
tremendous luck.

Or was it a dream? *Ordinary* people don't win the Gimcrack
Stakes, and become the guest of the Ancient Fraternité of
Gimcracks, and speak at the august and celebrated dinner. That's
for *them*, not us . . . for the Earls, and Dukes, and millionaires. The
ones who have *proper* horses.

But Tumbledownwind was a horse who made dreams come true
. . . a very special, once-in-a-lifetime equine David, who conquered
an army of Goliaths.

*Julian Wilson has been BBC Television racing correspondent since
1966 and prior to that he worked for seven years as a racing
journalist. His books include* Lester Piggott – The Pictorial
Biography, 100 Greatest Racehorses *and* The Racing World. *As
well as owning and breeding, he is a director of Seymour
Bloodstock, and operates as a racing manager.*

Peter Bromley
A PRIVATE VIEW OF COURAGE

With over thirty-seven years of racing to choose from and over 150 Classics commentated on for BBC radio, a wet, rainsoaked afternoon at an 'unfashionable' Goodwood meeting may seem an odd occasion to pick out as special. But in retrospect that awful or glorious day, depending on whether you were a bedraggled racegoer or, as in my case, a successful owner, still ranks as the most personally moving and important day in my short-lived career as a racehorse owner.

I became an owner when I came to know Ryan and Dorothy Price while I was writing Ryan's autobiography, *The Price of Success*. When we received our first advance on royalties, we decided to spend the money on buying a yearling. Treasury Bond was the first horse we bought and the manner of his acquisition makes strange telling.

At the previous December sales Ryan had been underbidder for a bonny little chestnut foal by one of his favourite stallions, Good Bond. He had lost the colt at 4,000 guineas but at the 1974 October sales here was this same fellow now offered as a yearling. Together we went to see him in his box; there was no attendant and we were both shocked at the condition of the colt. He stood in the box, head down, his coat dull and his ribs showing through his skin. Ryan spent a long time looking him over and outside the box he said 'I cannot understand it, he was a fine little foal, but all he wants is a good feed; we will get him cheap.' There was but one bid, Ryan's at 200 guineas, so at a cost of £108.00 including VAT, I owned half of the colt that we later called Treasury Bond, registered in partnership with Ryan's wife Dorothy.

Ryan, as usual, was quite right and during the winter at the Findon Academy for cheaply bought yearlings, Treasury Bond thrived and grew. At Brighton on 21 April he became Ryan's first two-year-old runner of 1975. When I saw the colt in the paddock I was both amazed and alarmed. He looked outstanding; his coat gleamed in the sun and he walked round the paddock as if he owned the place.

'Can he win?' I asked Ryan, for I had not even contemplated having a punt first time out.

'Not a hope, I haven't been able to do any work with him, the gallops have been waterlogged; but he's been through the traps once.'

In fact Treasury Bond, after being in last place at halfway, came up on us unfancied and unbacked at 12–1, beating three previous winners. Just eighteen days later at Lingfield, he justified being a short-priced favourite and strolled home by three lengths. Two out of two.

What should have been a glorious summer campaign with a tough and sound two-year-old now became a nightmare, for Findon was hit by a virus and throughout the months of June, July and August the double winner stayed at home. Treasury Bond reappeared at the Doncaster St Leger meeting and carried 8st 12lb to win the Rous Nursery at 8–1, again running unfancied. After being out of touch at halfway he ran on like a really good horse to get up by three-quarters of a length.

The Limekiln Stakes at Goodwood over seven furlongs in September was the race Ryan had earmarked for the colt's follow-up. As I drove through Alton on my way to the course, the water lying on the roads suggested abnormal rainfall. It was still raining when I arrived at Goodwood. Ryan looked up at the low clouds over Trundle Hill and said: 'This is just what your fellow wants.' It certainly was; all of Good Bond's stock needed cut in the ground; but I was extremely worried at the conditions of the race, for our colt had to give a stone or more away to all the other runners. As the ground became heavy, this seemed a daunting prospect.

Commentating on big races always puts one under some stress and pressure, but I have never felt as nervous before a commentary race as I did when Treasury Bond was running. At Goodwood that day, as the rain continued to pour down and both the lad leading up our colt and Norman Freeman the travelling head lad were absolutely soaked as the runners paraded, I felt sick with anxiety as

Tony Murray took the exceptionally keen Treasury Bond steadily down to the seven-furlong start and I made my way to the top of the grandstand just below my radio commentary box.

The mist and rain made it extremely hard to pick out the colours, but I saw my pale pink and grey silks shoot out of the stalls and lead the field; then, thank goodness, another horse took the lead and Tony Murray settled into second place. With misting-up race-glasses and shaking hands it was not easy to make sense of the race. As the runners came into the straight the leaders, which included Treasury Bond, all came over on to the stands side rails. Four furlongs out Treasury Bond was leading with the advantage of the rails. Now a challenger came up in the form of the grey Silver Steel and stuck to our horse with alarming determination. At one point, as Treasury Bond began to tire, the grey seemed to my eyes to be going slightly the better of the two, who by now had drawn ten lengths clear of the third horse.

Throughout the last furlong the two colts slogged it out and I felt that the concession of 14lb to the grey would swing the balance. I had not counted on the effectiveness of Tony Murray's finishing drive and our colt's quite astonishing bravery. What happened next transformed the finish of this race into an act of quite majestic courage, for Treasury Bond refused to be conquered; answering Tony Murray's calls, he rallied and got up to win by a head.

But as Tony Murray returned to the unsaddling enclosure his face told me a different story. 'I do not think I have won,' he said as he took off the saddle. While we waited anxiously for the result, Treasury Bond, leg-weary and dog-tired, stood quietly in the winner's enclosure. When the announcement came: 'First: number one', I simply could not believe it. This 200-guinea horse, trained by the master of Findon, had now won all four of the races that he had contested and but for the virus might have won several more. At Goodwood under 9st 6lb he had performed like a hero. Years later Tony Murray, with thousands of winners to his name, recalled the exact details of that win. He said, 'Treasury Bond that day on atrocious ground was one of the bravest horses that I ever rode.'

The Stewards abandoned the last two races as they considered that the ground was dangerous. I always have felt it a great injustice to Treasury Bond that his supreme performance as a two-year-old was witnessed by the smallest crowd that I have ever seen at

Goodwood. Peter Willett in the *Sporting Chronicle* headlined it: 'A STERLING VICTORY FOR TREASURY BOND'. He went on: 'Treasury Bond gave a performance to dream about in the Limekiln Stakes. Although he was giving at least a stone to each of his nine opponents and the going was terribly testing, he struggled on manfully to beat Silver Steel by a head after a ding-dong struggle which lasted for the whole of the last quarter mile.'

That was Treasury Bond's last race in Britain. During the winter he was sold to William Carl to race in the USA. He was actually entered for the Kentucky Derby but after running in a race at Arlington Park he broke a bone in his knee and never raced again.

He was allotted 8st 7lb in the Free Handicap and *Timeform* rated him at 113. Silver Steel became a very smart three-year-old handicapper, winning three races including the Rose of York Handicap at the York August meeting.

Many years later I learnt that as a yearling, while turned out in paddocks in Ireland, Treasury Bond had jumped several fences and joined some hunter mares, which he then proceeded to cover. No doubt had he won the Kentucky Derby some extremely well connected foals would have emerged.

I can recall so many exciting race days in my career, but the most vivid and moving was that damp day at Goodwood when Treasury Bond showed his true mettle and nobody saw it but me and a handful of racegoers.

Peter Bromley is BBC Radio's racing commentator. During his 33 years with the BBC, he has 'called live' over 5500 races, including some 150 Classics.

George Ennor
MONKEY

One of the several ways in which jumping scores over Flat racing is that it has avoided almost total domination by the big guns. Certainly Martin Pipe trains vast numbers of winners; for sure the large stables like those of David Elsworth, Nick Henderson, Arthur Stephenson, Oliver Sherwood and Gordon Richards win their share of the big races; but there is still, happily, a place for the one-man band. Can you imagine a Derby or a King George VI and Queen Elizabeth Stakes being won by a trainer with half a dozen horses? If you can you should tell the world that Hans Christian Andersen has been reincarnated in your form, but it requires no stretch of mind to envisage a Cheltenham Gold Cup hero being trained by a permit-holder. Sirrell Griffiths did so with Norton's Coin in 1990 and you can hardly claim that Arthur Barrow, who won with Master Smudge in 1980, was a major, fashionable name in racing circles.

The season after Master Smudge's Gold Cup triumph a Yorkshire farmer named George Mason finished eleventh in the list of leading owners thanks to the exploits of just three home-bred horses – Waggoners Walk, Trojan Walk and Master Brutus, trained on the family farm by his 25-year-old daughter Caroline. The horses' successes in that season included those of Waggoners Walk in the Kim Muir Chase at Cheltenham and of Master Brutus in the Midlands Grand National at Uttoxeter, but exciting though those occasions were they have to play second fiddle, in my memory at least, to the happenings at Cheltenham twelve months earlier when Waggoners Walk won the National Hunt Chase. The occasion was described by Iain Mackenzie in his *Hunter Chasers and Point-to-Pointers* annual as 'a lifetime's thrill for all concerned' and there were plenty of others who were not directly involved for whom the result was more than just a bit special.

My first involvement with the Mason family came via my colleague Colin Russell, who is married to Caroline's sister Patricia (a name by which very few ever address her). They very kindly invited me to stay for the York Ebor meeting in 1978 and tolerated me *in situ* for many York fixtures thereafter, and it was during one of those early visits – maybe even on the very first one – that I met Caroline, who was then about to take out a permit for the first time. That first season as the official trainer of her father's horses under Rules yielded no more than a few places, but the great day wasn't far away and on 19 October 1979 Trojan Walk won a novice chase at Market Rasen at 33–1 and Caroline Mason's name made its first appearance in the list of winning trainers. By now she had acquired the nickname of 'The Trainer' among family and friends and as Trojan Walk continued his winning ways his older half-brother Waggoners Walk embarked on the campaign which was to lead to Cheltenham glory.

The start could not have been less auspicious: Monkey, as Waggoners Walk was known in the yard, was hampered and fell at the very first fence in a maiden hunter chase at Leicester in February 1980. The gloom was soon dispelled, though. Five days afterwards Waggoners Walk ran third to the high-class hunter-chaser Queensberry Lad at Catterick; later in the month Caroline rode him to victory in the Ladies' Open at the Sinnington point-to-point; and by the time he had won a hunter chase at Market Rasen the preparations for Cheltenham were complete. All that remained was to win the race.

Things had worked out very much in Waggoners Walk's favour. Though he was not the fastest horse in the world and had sometimes been inclined to drop himself out beyond recall, he was an extremely reliable jumper, relished the heavy ground which was the order of the day at Cheltenham and would stay every yard of the four miles. Nor was what you might call the home team the only element to appreciate that Waggoners Walk had a serious chance in the longest race of the Festival; though he started only seventh best in the field of twenty-three he was as well backed as any of those who started at a shorter price than his 10–1.

Things really could not have gone more smoothly. Tony Fowler, who now trains a small string of jumpers in Leicestershire and was at the time the regular rider for the Mason horses, was able to settle

Monkey in towards the rear of the field, though with no danger of becoming disastrously detached, as Somerton Court and Dual Power made the early running. At about halfway Waggoners Walk started to move up towards the leaders and it was not only the fact that I had had a small each-way bet on him that got the adrenalin flowing. Monkey was going at least as well as any other runner and there were real prospects that I was about to be involved, even if only on the fringe, with a Cheltenham winner.

Those hopes rose higher as Waggoners Walk went to the front six fences from home and down the hill to the third last he came gradually but inexorably clear. At the second last he was far enough in front for it to look inevitable that he would win – as long as he jumped the last. Jumping fences had never been a problem, and nor was it here; but four miles in testing ground were beginning to tell. That famous Cheltenham hill has seen many a drama over the years and as Weymouth Road started to close in the last 100 yards the cheers that had been so confident only a few seconds earlier took on a hint of desperation.

All was well, though. Waggoners Walk held on to win by a length and, at the age of 24, Caroline Mason had become one of the youngest, if not *the* youngest, person to train a winner at the Cheltenham Festival. It was a result received with considerable pleasure all round – not all the beaming faces at the unsaddling enclosure belonged to those who were directly involved.

The major celebrations came later in the year. On the night of the race itself Caroline and George Mason drove Waggoners Walk home in the horsebox, reaching the farm at East Heslerton Wold, off the A64 between Malton and Scarborough, at 2 a.m. at the end of an utterly memorable day. Twelve months later Waggoners Walk returned to Cheltenham and won the Kim Muir by thirty lengths. That was another great occasion; but nothing has yet equalled the magic feeling of that first Cheltenham success. Very little could.

George Ennor joined the Sporting Life *in 1960. He became chief reporter on that paper during his 25 years there, before moving to a similar position at the* Racing Post *when that paper was launched.*

Richard Baerlein
'NOW IS THE TIME TO BET LIKE MEN'

In the summer of 1980 Tim Neligan, managing director of United Racecourses, asked me if there was any chance of the *Guardian* newspaper sponsoring a horse race. In particular he suggested the Classic Trial at Sandown as most suitable because it practically advertised itself. In that year Henbit, having won the Trial, went on to win the Derby, following the example of Troy the year before; while in 1978 Shirley Heights had been second in the Sandown race and then won the Derby. I could not have had any stronger ammunition to present even to the most anti-racing board of directors in the land. The idea appealed to me greatly because I had enjoyed my association with two previous sponsorships involving the *Observer* Gold Cup and the Playboy Club. And sponsorships can be a great help to a working journalist in providing extra copy.

I obtained the *Observer* race through my association with Phil Bull, who founded the Timeform Gold Cup but after four years decided to give it up, claiming he had already had from it all the mileage available to his firm. However, Phil did think the race was of sufficient importance for it to be taken over by General Harding, the then chairman of the Levy Board. General Harding might have been prepared to do so on his own account, but strong pressure had been brought to bear on him from the Jockey Club, who were against the race – chiefly because it was not run at Newmarket. To say Phil was disgusted at the treatment of his brainchild was the understatement of the year. The *Observer* Gold Cup was perhaps the best sponsorship of all, but owing to union trouble the *Observer* gave it up after the 1975 running.

Alan Kinghorn, racing director of the Playboy Club, called me in to help with improving the Playboy interest and we had built up to fifteen sponsored races by the time the club was closed down.

165

So in 1980 I was ripe for a new sponsorship. I knew there would be no problem with Peter Gibbings (now Sir Peter), chairman of Guardian Newspapers. I had worked with him before when taking over the *Observer* Gold Cup at a time when he was assistant general manager of that paper. Peter was mad keen on racing; but could he convince a board whose paper did not have a racing column before he joined them and set one up in 1968 of the value of such a sponsorship? He liked the idea from the start, but warned me of the difficulties he would come up against when he presented the case to the board. He felt that there was only a 50–50 chance of success. You can imagine my delight when he told me the proposition that the *Guardian* sponsor the Classic Trial had been accepted by the board.

This is the background to a most enjoyable day's racing at Sandown on 25 April 1981, and if I did not bore you with the build-up you would not have known how it came to pass. Even better was to come when our first winner Shergar went on to win the Derby.

I had three reasons for delight that day. I had put the readers of the *Guardian* and the *Observer* on at 25–1 and 20–1, it fully justified the *Guardian* sponsorship for which I felt entirely responsible, and my own personal bank balance was given a boost.

There were many who thought that because my home was called 'Shergar' I had won enough on the horse to buy the house. I would like to put the matter right before we go any further. I had been farming, stud running and race-writing since the war but found the combination of jobs increasingly tiring. Therefore in 1981 we sold the farm and a beautiful small herd of Charolais and were looking for a place on the coast. Tony Murray wanted to sell his mother's house in Middleton and suggested my wife should pay a visit. Mrs Murray's house would need too much doing to it for us, but on the trip my wife passed a house nearing completion which attracted her attention. Within five days we had bought it, and as it was Shergar's year and he had been a great asset to me it was natural to name the house after the record-breaking ten-length Derby winner.

Shergar had been a useful two-year-old, winning on his debut the Haynes, Hanson and Clark maiden over a mile at Newbury, famous for producing Derby winners; but had been beaten two-and-a-half lengths by Beldale Flutter next time out in the William Hill Futurity.

The official handicappers did not rate that race very highly and Shergar was only given 8st 9lb in the Free Handicap. Actually the race proved one of the best in the series, apart from the Vaguely Noble and Noblesse victories, for Beldale Flutter won the Mecca-Dante and Benson and Hedges, Shergar won his first five and the fourth horse, Recitation, won the French Two Thousand Guineas. However, after publication of the Free Handicap weights there was no rush to back Shergar for the Derby and 33–1 was freely offered. Moreover, Walter Swinburn and his father Wally went off for a winter holiday in India both convinced that Centurius would be Walter's Derby mount.

In the spring rumours began suggesting Shergar had wintered exceptionally well and he soon became one of those noted as possible winners of the first *Guardian* sponsorship. In both the *Guardian* and the *Observer* I suggested that if he won that race he would become favourite for the Derby. He did win it, and by ten lengths at even money, but when I rang up several bookmakers on the Sunday before describing the race for *Guardian* readers on Monday morning I was told he stood at 8–1, for there were still those who thought Walter might ride Centurius. My report included 'that at 8–1 Shergar for the Derby, now is the time to bet like men'. Ladbrokes among others have never forgotten that race and Ron Pollard reminds me of it whenever I meet him.

It was a wonderful afternoon at Sandown as Shergar was led into the unsaddling enclosure followed by his owner the Aga Khan, for whom it was also a special occasion. Shergar was one of the first yearlings he sent to England after deciding in 1978 to follow the example of his father and grandfather by having horses trained in this country. The *Guardian* had entertained a large number of guests, most of whom knew little or nothing about racing, but they had had it well drummed into them in the sports pages of the *Guardian* that morning that Shergar was going to win. We were over the first hurdle and the *Guardian* racing sponsorship was away to a flying start.

When Walter Swinburn entered Michael Stoute's stables at the end of 1980 he had only been a jockey for two-and-a-half years and was only 19 at the time; but Centurius was still to be reckoned with as the colt who, in his first race as a three-year-old, had beaten Robellino in the Blue Riband Trial at Epsom.

At the Chester meeting that followed, the first two in the *Guardian* race came out with flying colours, Shergar winning the Vase by twelve lengths and Kirtling, ten lengths behind Shergar at Sandown, winning the Dee Stakes by six lengths: so there was no chance of the form being out of place. Immediately after his Chester victory Shergar was momentarily laid at 9–2 but from then on he steadily hardened until his final starting price was 11–10 on. There did not appear to be any danger to Shergar from any quarter, though the public would support Lester Piggott on Shotgun who had been beaten three-quarters of a length by Beldale Flutter in the Dante.

One tends to become nervous as the great occasion approaches, but in expecting an even more outstanding day than at Sandown I wrote in anticipation of success: 'it would be hard to find a more stoutly built Classic colt with a better pedigree. The way he went round Chester suggested he would even be at home in a five-furlong event at the Calgary Stampede.'

On the Monday morning 0.63 inches of rain fell, leaving the going soft: exactly to Shergar's requirements.

The victory of Shergar was a very special moment for me, even though the pressure of Derby Day with an article to prepare for the next day's edition of the paper gave me no time to relax or celebrate the victory. It was the culmination of events which had been building up over the last few months; and it justified everything we had said and done. There was not a single person in the *Guardian* building who could disagree with the management's decision to go ahead with the sponsorship. It had been an outstanding success.

When the *Observer* had to give up the sponsorship of the Gold Cup in 1976, John Hislop estimated the advertising value of the race at £250,000. What can the value of the Classic Trial be today? I am proud to have been associated with two such projects.

Richard Baerlein joined the Sporting Chronicle *in 1936 and the* Evening Standard *after the Second World War. He has written for the* Observer *since 1963 and was the* Guardian's *first racing correspondent in 1968. He was a stud owner and breeder of racehorses and Charolais cows until 1982.*

Wheels of fortune

Tony Stafford
THE RETURN OF THE MAESTRO

Where were you when you heard about it?

Not President Kennedy's assassination, although I can still recall that minute of history as vividly as if it were a week ago.

No, I'm talking about one of those rare moments when something unthinkable happens.

I was at home on a Thursday evening when the office called to say Lester Piggott was making his riding comeback at the age of 54 years and 300-odd days. Impossible? Not according to the *Daily Telegraph*'s editor Max Hastings, who'd actually alerted us to the unlikely possibility seven months earlier. Max had been at a dinner, apparently seated next to a Jockey Club member who said that Lester was planning a comeback. As a result of that dinner conversation, I had been detailed to phone Newmarket on the Wednesday of the Cheltenham Festival; this I did, fully expecting a blank wall to be erected against what I felt was a silly enquiry.

Picture my face, then, when the great man himself came on the phone. And it wasn't just a 30-second call; it lasted the entire time it took 66–1 chance New Halen to win the last race on the card that Cheltenham Wednesday. The bare bones of our chat, apart from some pleasantries concerning mutual acquaintances, were that he had no plans to return to the saddle, a message I was happy to convey confidently to my editor.

Seven months later the self-same Max Hastings let it be known that he wasn't exactly thrilled with my bash at investigative journalism. Clearly some hasty retrieval work was called for.

On the Friday morning I got through to Lester. He could not have been more co-operative, and this despite the hordes of pressmen and photographers outside the door – almost like the days a couple of years earlier when he faced an imminent prison sentence for tax offences. Happily, Lester agreed to write a first-person piece in the next Monday's paper outlining his thoughts on returning after almost five years away from the job he had performed with such exquisite style since 1948, when as a 12-year-old he rode his first winner at Haydock Park. As part of the same deal, the financial aspect of which would not have paid for a paragraph of a Paul Gascoigne interview, Lester also agreed to write an article on his comeback day at Leicester, and agreed that I could travel there with him in the car.

We assembled in Hamilton Road, Newmarket, mid-morning for the drive to the Midlands, Lester in the front seat and Bryn Crossley, who had been associated with the Piggott stable ever since the former champion's original retirement in 1985, taking the wheel of the Piggott Mercedes. That, too, was a pleasant coincidence for the day's back-seat passenger: a decade earlier I had booked rides for the young Mr Crossley during the season when he collected the apprentices' trophy. Fate had not always dealt the best of cards to Bryn since then, but there are few more optimistic characters around racing and his non-stop repartee kept the atmosphere light all the way, despite endless traffic delays.

Leicester's car park is the ideal site for a fifth-rate car boot sale, but hardly the appropriate landing place for a major media event of this nature, and the Piggott party of one large, one medium and one small (Mr Crossley) person got almost to the gates before being recognized.

Lester was unsure how he would be received, but his arrival at the entrance immediately allayed any fears that the public would share the hostility of some sections of the sports press (though not, I must emphasize, the racing press). Cameras clicked, video recorder units whirred, the cheers of enthusiasts who had come from all over the country rang out – and Lester's smile told those near enough to see it that he had something to live for again.

Soon, in the colours of his great friend Charles St George, he demonstrated that the years had not diminished his talent, which remained unique. His rival jockeys seemed to bask in the reflected glory. Racing was news for the right reasons again.

The record books will state that Lupescu, owned by Mr St George and trained by Henry Cecil, was beaten a short head, but the perfect, sympathetic ride which this newcomer received from the maestro was the distillation of more than forty years' experience.

Lester had two more rides, both unplaced; as the runners were prepared for the race in which he was to have his last mount of the day, Patricia, the wheels were already turning in his shrewd head. As he and Crossley – riding in the race for the Piggott stable – came out, Bryn thrust the car keys into my hand. We'd arranged a quick getaway to avoid another impromptu press conference: Lester had already held court in the winner's enclosure after his first ride. As the runners pulled up, I was to collect the car and drive it round to another exit behind the Racecourse Technical Services van, which Lester and Bryn would reach after a dash out of the back door of the weighing room.

After finding the mechanism to push the seat back a few inches to accommodate my bulk – Bryn had reckoned I'd put on five stone since the days I was helping him – I turned the key in the ignition and got no response. Despite its being mid-October and quite cool, the sweat began to pour down my neck as I envisaged Lester left in the open at the mercy of a pack of ravenous newshounds. It was not until about the tenth attempt that I realized the car *had* started, the quiet hum of the engine passing unnoticed behind the panicky panting of an unfit and anxious driver.

Fortunately for my own self-esteem, the car reached the arranged spot just as the jockeys emerged, and they were in place in time to get a start on a camera crew in full flight with journalist Graham Rock in the vanguard. The traffic by now had swollen as Lester devotees left the track, and Rock saw his chance. He knocked on the window, thrusting a microphone into a two-inch gap at the top.

'Come on, Lester, give us a word,' Rock pleaded. Being a novice in such matters, I suggested it might be an idea. Wickedly, with a smirk on the old stoneface, Lester said, 'Tell him you've bought me exclusively,' which was laughable considering what he could have demanded for the story if commercial considerations had applied.

Meanwhile, autograph hunters were better received and a string of attractive young ladies secured the coveted scrawl while their husbands and boyfriends queued to leave the track.

I thought I'd be driving all the way and was just getting used to the car when Lester said: 'Pull over in that garage, Bryn can drive.'

There was an atmosphere of satisfaction all the way back to Newmarket, where we conducted our interview. The words that went into the paper were almost entirely his own, in notable contradiction of the carping comments made by some of the better regarded sports journalists who reckoned (wrongly) that he could not put two words together. It would have been salutary for them to have witnessed a remarkable scene the following evening after he had returned in triumph from his first two wins at Chepstow.

We flew down to Badminton and took a taxi across the bridge to Chepstow, where he won on Nicholas, trained by his wife Susan for Henryk de Kwiatkowski. Apart from Lester and me, the other passenger was a most reluctant Joe Oliver, the stable's head lad, whose fear of flying is legendary. Luckily the elements were kind, the pilot Neil on form and the journey uneventful, except to show the best of the English countryside at unaccustomedly close range.

Nicholas, favourite for the Biddestone All-Aged Stakes, won well by half a length at 6–4 on from Amigo Menor and Lester came back to a rousing Welsh welcome. This time the sports boys had other things to attend to, like advising the England soccer manager on who should be in and out of his next team; and it was the close racing set who were able to enjoy the moment.

But to return to the scene in the Piggott sitting-room. We were running dangerously close to the paper's bedtime, and Lester's first-person report on how he'd done it was still unwritten. So after a few perfunctory questions, I settled down to ad lib, with the qualification that he might interject if I said anything he didn't agree with. We'd gone a few words talking to the telephonist at the *Daily Telegraph* when he suddenly stopped me.

'Tell him to wait a minute,' he said. 'Say . . .' and so it went on for the next half an hour or so. Every word was measured and qualified, and if the result may not have been one of the world's greatest journalistic achievements, it was from the heart of a happy man.

And for me, the memory as I assess another hundred or so Piggott winners in the interim? The simplicity, sincerity and strength of the man. He'd seen the bottom and was going back to the top with just his talent, toughness and the admiration of the public who'd known him for ever.

Comebacks like his can never be bettered. I feel very, very lucky to have shared a tiny part of this one.

Tony Stafford, 46, has been on the racing staff at the Daily Telegraph *for 20 years. He was racing editor from 1979 to 1990 and is now racing correspondent.*

Monty Court
GEORGE WALKS TALL

At 6ft 1in in his socks George Spann wasn't designed for scuttling around at dwarf height; but that's how he used to enter the Midland Bank, Swindon, to avoid catching the manager's eye.

As times got worse George's stooped visits became regular Friday morning expeditions to draw money from an account so long overdrawn that black ink was a remote memory. The sense of relief when he straightened up outside, with money in his pocket, only temporarily eased the tensions and frustrations brought on by bad luck nobbling his runners and owners not paying their bills.

Back in his yard at Lambourn his horses looked well. They always did, but even the best seemed to have incurable seconditis, and backing them to get enough to pay the wages (and avoid the dreaded bank run) was proving increasingly disastrous.

But George was never short on optimism and when he set off for Aintree on 27 March 1969 he had genuine and realistic hopes that his handsome, game mare La Ina, who had never fallen in her life, would bring the bad run to an end – even if it was in a race as tough and competitive as the Topham over two miles and five furlongs of the Grand National course in the days when Aintree was no place for fainthearts.

On the principle that desperate situations need desperate measures George rustled up as much money as he could, sent up a silent prayer, and had a hefty bet at 100–7.

His spirits were given a much-needed boost by the realization that La Ina looked a picture as she left the parade ring with substitute jockey Bill Rees on her back, and that she was by far the best looking and best turned out in a field of twenty.

In the race she always seemed to be travelling comfortably and was in fourth place at the Canal Turn, although she then lost her place slightly and slipped back. When the field entered the straight, however, the ten- year-old started to make ground on the leaders at a rate so impressive that she looked to have a stone in hand. But La Ina was always a law unto herself and had to be allowed to jump fences her way; and when Bill Rees tried to organize her at the second last, she hit it with such force that sprigs of spruce became jammed under her girths. It was a miracle she stayed on her feet, let alone that Rees was able to stay in the saddle to gather her up and continue the challenge.

This earthquake of a mistake cost them the race, for even though La Ina finished like the proverbial train she was unable to peg back a length and a half on the winner Dozo at the line. Once again a George Spann runner was an unlucky second. And this was no year to be making mistakes against the Toby Balding–Eddie Harty combination of Dozo because they were to win the Grand National a couple of days later with Highland Wedding.

On the long journey back to Lambourn, George had plenty of time to think about his problems: the ever-growing overdraft, the fates that seemed to conspire to keep his runners out of the winner's enclosure; and the owners who wouldn't pay their bills. One man owed £8,000 in a total of some £17,000 outstanding. In 1969 that was serious money.

Although they had enjoyed their good days and some big winners, life seemed to have worked out an equation that meant that the harder the Spanns worked, the harder Lady Luck kicked them in the teeth. George was stating no more than the obvious when he told his travelling companions that he was fed up with the game and was going to sell up and get out.

Word couldn't have spread around the Lambourn racing community faster if he had called a press conference. Within twenty-four hours Stan Mellor, looking for a place to train at the end of a momentous twenty-year riding career, was on the phone. In a matter of weeks Faringdon Road Stables had become Linkslade, new home of the Mellor family and named after a horse on which the three-times champion Stan had ridden fifteen of his 1,035 winners.

And so at the age 54 George moved to Ireland where he bought a run-down 40-acre farm on the outskirts of the historic town of Kells, Co. Meath, some 45 miles north-west of Dublin. The plan was a stud farm.

He took with him one of his chasing heroines Another Rose (later to become dam of the classy chaser Lastofthebrownies), and an ex-Flat filly Maggie's Pet, both already in foal to Klondyke Bill. La Ina and other mares joined them later.

Months of back-breaking slog turned the fields into immaculate post-and-railed paddocks. Farm buildings and barns were converted into the finest boxes in the district. And the house and garden were transformed into visions worthy of a glossy magazine feature.

On 22 September 1971 George Spann's spruced-up Grangegodden Stud sold its first yearlings – the two Klondyke Bills. Maggie's Pet's son sold for £400 and was destined to earn a huge punters' following as the prolific sprinter Maxi's Taxi, while Another Rose's son sold for £1,450.

A few more years of hard work, some successful pinhooking and the sale of some modest but immaculately turned out homebred yearlings was no recipe for riches, but for the first time in years George found that he could walk into his bank measuring his full height.

This new-found confidence enabled him to go to Ballsbridge Sales and bid for a well-bred mare culled by the McGrath family's Brownstown Stud in the confident style of a man with a very fat wallet and the sky as his limit.

In reality he had already reached his maximum when the seven-year-old Pardao mare Demare was knocked down to him for 3,000 guineas. She was in foal to the first-season stallion Ballymore who had won the Irish Two Thousand Guineas on his very first racecourse appearance.

It wasn't only Spann's brisk bidding that sealed the day. The brown mare didn't appeal to any but the most serious bloodline student: she looked trouble as she struggled round the ring with a deformed joint that was the hangover of a training injury. But George was so pleased with his day's work that he walked into Demare's box when he got her home and hung his arms around her neck.

Spann's care and the skills of his vet Joe Clarke ensured that the hugely swollen joint never seriously troubled her in the years ahead, and in the following spring she gave birth to a brown filly foal who was jumping and kicking half an hour after coming into the world.

I got to know 'Bally' well in the months ahead. When she was old enough she spent plenty of time with her mother in the same paddock as my filly – although she left the lumbering Crystal Court for dead when she lowered herself and stretched out in a gallop.

In September 1976 we loaded 'Bally' and a pinhooked Jukebox filly into the trailer and set off for the Goffs yearling sale at Kill, where George persuaded his old friend Paddy Prendergast, who had trained Ballymore, to look at her. He bought her for 3,000 guineas.

The following May, when George and I were at The Curragh for the Guineas meeting, Paddy met George outside the weighing room and told him of his high hopes for 'the best filly in the yard who will win first time out – and a Classic next year'. Her name: More So, alias 'Bally'.

It wasn't just the champagne that made George starry-eyed. Back at Grangegodden we made a bee-line for Demare's box and gazed at her with big grins as we fed her apples. After all, she was not only tipped by one of the best judges in the world to be the dam of one of next year's Classic winners, but her belly was fat with a full-brother or sister.

September came and Paddy, true to his word, produced More So at The Curragh to win in such impressive style that soon the whole Irish racing community was talking of her as a future Classic winner. That's why, the following spring, she started as 2–1 co-favourite for the Irish One Thousand Guineas without having set foot on a racecourse for eight months.

It was a day when I broke the rules by taking George, already white-faced and shellshocked by the occasion, into the Curragh press box in the hope that he would relax and watch his big moment in comfort.

A furlong out More So burst into the lead. Suddenly the pale, tense, silent ghost at my side started to roar and punch the air so violently that three Dublin racing journalists were not only deafened but knocked off balance. They were only slightly placated by learning that the madman in their midst had got another filly at home 'just like the winner' – and another on the way.

I have never been able to remember whether we drank more champagne or lemonade because of the stops on the way back to Grangegodden to pour huge quantities of lemonade into Spann to sober him up in time for dinner.

Demare's breeding career was to ensure more champagne and

lemonade days, and was best described by Tony Morris in 1982 when George told him after selling a Habitat half-brother to More So for £370,000: 'It beats training unlucky selling-platers for owners who don't pay their bills.'

Friday, 12 May 1978 was the day that changed it all . . . even though it tends to get misty round the edges. It was certainly the greatest racing day of my life. More importantly, it was the day that guaranteed that George Spann, unassuming horsemaster, could walk tall for the rest of his.

Monty Court was not merely bitten but savaged by the racing bug when the Evening Avertiser, *Swindon, wanted a story of local runners in the 1949 Grand National. He successfully edited the* Sporting Life *for five years when the* Racing Post *was launched, and now writes a weekly column for the paper.*

Ivor Herbert
THE LUCK OF THE GOLD CUP

In the sweat and slap of Cheltenham's tacky old winner's enclosure, they asked me: 'When did you think you'd win the Gold Cup?' I said, ''Bout halfway up the hill.' I felt extraordinarily calm, as if suspended in post-accident shock. The luck, the many aspects of good fortune leading on from one event to another, seemed impossible to credit. But luck rules racing. And it runs all through this story.

I added politely, 'Linny has to come with a late run, you see. That's why.' But they were interested in other, easier things about the winner's past and future.

Yet it was the lateness of Linwell's brilliant final burst which, for his two previous seasons, had kept him ahead of the handicapper. So he had climbed from winning Sandown's Mildmay Memorial off 9st 9lb in 1956 to winning the Gold Cup only fourteen months later. He won his races very late and often by very little. In that respect he was a trainer's joy. And by those seemingly slow improvements he had crept up in class, granting us droplets of hope. It meant he progressed as all horses should: starting low, improving steadily, never being overfaced until each rung had been climbed. No racehorse should be daunted by man's over-optimism. The deep end must wait.

I was there in the winner's enclosure shamefully hatless. In 1957 hats were as *de rigueur* as trousers. Bowler hats, even, were worn by the old brigade. But I had flung my battered Herbert Johnson brown job high into the grey sky as Linny left his cousin Kerstin one length behind at the post. No one ever saw it descend. But the good hatters, reading of the miraculous ascension, swiftly, kindly sent me another.

In the photographs I look like a child surrounded by old men.

Michael Dickinson, who I thought was younger than I was when he won his first Gold Cup, says that at 31, I just beat him. He's usually right on facts. Here are senior trainers like Fred and Mercy Rimell (who had run ESB), Verly Bewicke, always sporting, whose Kerstin we had yet again beaten, congratulating me and thrilled Charlie Mallon, my little rosy-cheeked head lad, who only came racing to Cheltenham, and then only if we expected a winner. Ten years earlier he had been head lad to Hector Christie when Fortina won the race. Lofty Peter Cazalet, who trained the third, Rose Park, said something courteously kind. Dour Alec Kilpatrick, whose Pointsman, fourth, had beaten us before, as usual said nothing, but may have grunted.

So I wondered, now levitated by elation and a warming awareness of triumph, when it was that I had truly thought that such an amazing thing might come to pass. At Christmas we certainly nurtured strong hopes. But then, hopes for horses generally shrink the closer you get to the off. The smallish brown gelding with the broad white blaze had won another four 'chases in succession. We had one of our rare bets. A fading sepia card from Fred Binns Ltd – that *real* bookmaker Ted Sturman (such sportsmen are worlds away from BOLA's greedy crew) is stuck in Linwell's portrait in the hall. It says baldly that I was £1,312 10s in credit. That was our December ante-post, worth I suppose some £15,000 in today's cash. It was only a little less than my annual salary from the *Evening News*, the agreeable racing and horsey job which (since I had deserted supposedly high prospects in the boring City) led to my trainer's licence being held in the name of wise old Charlie Mallon.

But when I bought the horse, one long Yeatsian summer evening in Tipperary, I hadn't even planned to run him under Rules at all. His purchaser, my owner David Brown, maker of gears, tractors, Lagondas, Aston Martins and many pounds, wanted to set up a little point-to-point stable on his new farm at Cadmore End in the Chilterns. I was to buy a couple of young horses – 'top price £750, Ivor, mind' – qualify and point-to-point them.

At first David Brown held the permit while I, before going to the City, trained a couple of old and unsound jumpers he had brought down from Yorkshire. Though I rose over seven years to be nominally the assistant MD of the Charterhouse Finance

Corporation, the prospects never pleased me at all. But to buy, train and ride a few more point-to-pointers, and at someone else's expense . . . bliss! It was lucky I had already met David Brown in the City when Charterhouse floated his Corporation. And luck in timing too, that I'd by then ridden some point-to-point winners in the Midlands.

Fortune favoured even the purchase. To buy potential jumpers then I combed the Irish form-book for horses who had run a few times, but improvingly, in bumper races and who were privately trained. I would then ask that famous jockey, dapper Aubrey Brabazon (still riding in those days) if he knew the horses and whether they might be bought.

Thus one August evening to an out-farm belonging to the formidable Mr Paddy Quinn of Kilbragh, Tipperary, within a few miles of Vincent O'Brien, still active on the jumping front with the likes of Saffron Tartan. Mr Quinn had sold Golden Miller and the winners of every Grand National bar the Welsh.

He wanted £1,500 for Linwell. I had half that to spend.

The shadows lengthened. Back up in Wicklow my house party was going off to a glittering ball. We walked around and around the track through the thistly field where Linwell was trained. Paddy Quinn swished the grasses with his heavy stick. I had been captivated by the bold activity of the horse. With the optimism of youth I felt even the flinty Chilterns provided more facilities than these poor fields. Suddenly Mr Quinn thrust out a great hand.

'The horse is yours. I like you.'

With the vet's report, another touch of luck. He failed him for his wind. But wise old men in Leicestershire had told me that 'high blowers' never went in their wind. And how he high-blew! In races the opposition could hear him coming and quake. I over-ruled the vet and chanced it.

Linwell proved a potty hunter. Leaning forwards once to unhook a gate with the South Oxfordshire, I felt the sky spin. Linny had jumped five bars from a stand. Then in the spring came greater luck out of apparent adversity: racing's recurrent silver lining. David Brown had a notion that racehorses could be taught jumping only by being lunged, unridden, over a fixed pole. It's an excellent education which I subsequently used for years. But, I tried to tell Brown, you do need to school horses at speed. We hadn't.

After falling with Linwell at the first fence in his first point-to-point at Crowell, I schooled him daily across the farm, and ran him at Lockinge in a large race, later described by *Horse and Hound* as 'the best point-to-point ever'. To survive, I hacked him round behind. And so, by luck, we discovered how to ride him. After two miles I came up with a friend, John Heyworth.

'How many ahead?' I asked.

'A dozen.'

I kicked. Linwell's acceleration was such that, as Fred Winter was astonished to discover years later at Newbury, the pilot very nearly fell out of the back of the saddle. Thus, hard held, we finished a close third to two good horses and I thought we would probably win our Hunt Race next time out. But by kindly fate, he had lanced a sprig of birch into his elbow (he always jumped with forelegs well up). Thankfully it went septic. So, joyfully, he missed the rest of the season. If he had not, he would have continued for years to carry me bumbling round in point-to-points, his immense talent unsuspected beneath my incompetence.

Instead, professionally ridden, he ran over hurdles in the autumn and often nearly won. I switched him to fences and here again, luck leapt out of adversity's shadow. Tommy Cusack, a good jockey who lived nearby, had been schooling him over fences. Suddenly, in Kempton's changing room on the afternoon of Linwell's first steeplechase, he told me, 'I can't ride that novice today. I've got Cheltenham to think of. But, look, I've got so-and-so for you.'

'No, thanks,' said I. I was standing next to Michael Scudamore whose riding style I had long admired. 'Would you. . . ?', I asked diffidently.

And so began, by almost sheer chance, the partnership which took us to the Gold Cup.

Even at next day's dawn it was so hard to believe that, after the Rimells had royally entertained us, we had to tiptoe into Linwell's box to touch him to reassure ourselves that he was real. As usual, for he was a fiercely testy character when fully fit, who much preferred his own company, he made as if to nip me.

The race remains my most measurable moment of triumph. I've occasionally had books in the best-selling lists. But there's no instant victory there; only encouraging noises to say they're doing well. Nothing compares with that small brown battling horse, as much a part of me as my arm or head, going past the post in front, victorious after four years' dreaming. This must be the motivation which makes less lucky trainers and owners go on desperately hoping.

Even today, it's hard to credit that golden chain of lucky links. The horse nearly won the next two Gold Cups, too: blundered and unseated rider in 1958, and in 1959 second when stopped to a halt by Pas Seul falling across him at the last. John Welcome in his *The Cheltenham Gold Cup* writes: 'In the history of this race Linwell must go down as one of the unlucky horses . . . Had the wheel of fortune turned even slightly his way after his first victory, he would almost certainly have figured in the record books as the winner of three Gold Cups.'

Probably, unbelievably right. But, oh, how that wheel of fortune turned for him and for me in the years before.

Ivor Herbert has published 25 books, was a City executive, is a scriptwriter for theatre, cinema and TV, trained NH horses, has a small video company, runs a wine firm, and is senior travel writer and racing editor of the Mail on Sunday.

John de Moraville
AINTREE AGONY AND ECSTASY

'And it's Red Rum and Tommy Stack now from Churchtown Boy, The Pilgarlic and Eyecatcher as they come to the last fence of the National, Red Rum with a tremendous chance of winning his third National.

'He jumps it clear of Churchtown Boy. He is getting the most tremendous cheer from the crowd. They are willing him home now.

'The twelve-year-old Red Rum being preceded only by loose horses, being chased by Churchtown Boy. Eyecatcher has moved into third and The Pilgarlic fourth.

'They are coming to the elbow. There is a furlong now between Red Rum and his third Grand National triumph and he is coming up to the line to win it like a fresh horse, to win it in great style.

'It's hats off, a tremendous reception. You have never heard the like of it at Liverpool. Red Rum wins the National.'

What a crescendo. Peter O'Sullevan's famous commentary could almost have lifted Red Rum home on its own! As Peter's assistant, high in the grandstand, inches from the great 'Voice' himself, I can vouch for the wholesale euphoria. Crowds below us went mad. I, truly, had never heard the like of it at Liverpool . . . or anywhere else.

Yet it was with decidedly mixed feelings that, having scribbled on my racecard the first four home, checked any late fallers and noted the pulled-ups that were hacking safely home, I scanned Aintree's vast acres in search of two special horses that, apparently, had failed to finish.

Both were trained by Peter Bailey and had set out carrying the striking black-and-white colours of that most enthusiastic of owners, Michael Buckley. Bailey, my half-brother, trained then at Sparsholt in Oxfordshire, barely a mile from my home, and I took a

185

keen interest in all his runners. You can imagine the excitement of a smallish stable saddling two fancied starters in the world's greatest steeplechase. Though no Red Rums, they both went to Liverpool with sporting chances and were bracketed in the betting at 18–1. Prince Rock, giving everything under a whip-brandishing Graham Thorner, had been beaten a heart-breaking half-length in Cheltenham's National Hunt (now Ritz Club) Handicap Chase, while Zeta's Son was one of the country's top staying handicappers, boasting stylish wins in both the Hennessy Gold Cup and the Anthony Mildmay Peter Cazalet Memorial. I had missed Zeta's finest hour, opting, instead of the Hennessy, for the delights of Camden, South Carolina, where stable-companion The Bo-Weevil (ridden, incidentally, by Red Rum's partner Tommy Stack) had attempted, unavailingly, to lift the Colonial Cup International Chase. It was still a tremendous thrill to cheer home the victorious Grand Canyon (Ron Barry) – and an even greater one when we learnt the news from Newbury.

Right now, though, the news at Aintree, as thousands of Red Rum fans poured off the stands and advanced on the ancient winner's enclosure, was, for me, becoming less euphoric by the second.

My role, after leaving O'Sullevan's box, is to battle my way towards the door of the weighing room – a more gruelling assault course than the National itself! – and there check with each returning jockey where he finished, capsized or pulled up. That not always straightforward exercise is for the benefit of BBC *Grandstand* which, after interviewing the winning owner, trainer, jockey, lad, etc., tabulates the finishing order, pinpointing for the once-a-year punters exactly where they did their money.

It transpired that Prince Rock's National had ended at the twelfth fence and that, mercifully, he was unscathed. The fate and whereabouts of Zeta's Son, though, remained a mystery. As the sound barriers succumbed to Red Rum celebrations my anxiety for Zeta's Son's safety heightened. Watching much of the race on a television monitor, I was not certain that he had fallen. But his jockey Mouse Morris (now such a successful trainer) had not returned, and the omens were not good.

Later, Mouse, looking dazed and dejected, slipped almost unnoticed through the teeming multitudes – who had eyes and ears for only one horse – into the safe haven of the weighing room. Zeta's Son had fallen at Valentine's Brook second time round and – much worse than that – had broken a leg. It was the news I dreaded. But during the almost endless waiting I had started to suspect it.

Red Rum's third Grand National win – a history-making performance virtually certain never to be repeated – suddenly became almost an irrelevance. Here I was at the heart of one of the greatest sporting achievements of all time . . . yet celebration was the last thing on my mind.

I should have been privileged to be at Aintree that first Saturday of April 1977. Apart from Rummy's road to glory, the whole card was of the highest quality and had already thrown up two results to savour. Mouse Morris had warmed up for the National in the best possible style driving the Irish-trained Skymas, the dual Two-Mile Champion, to a courageous win under 12st top weight in the Sun Ratings Chase. This was one of the most exhilarating performances of the season and a spectacular curtain-raiser. But, amazingly, it was eclipsed just half an hour later when Night Nurse and Monksfield battled head to head for the line in a Templegate Hurdle epic. The judge was unable to separate them and, as the tension mounted to a fever pitch only Red Rum could surpass, he announced a dead heat.

That could not have been a fairer result, as the first and second in the Champion Hurdle each gave their very last ounce, Night Nurse responding to Paddy Broderick's frenzied urgings to share the honours in what was the most thrilling finish of the season. Little Monksfield (Dessie Hughes) had joined the front-running Night Nurse after the third last flight, where a bad mistake brought the champ back to the field. The 'big two' then matched strides all the way to the line. No one dared guess which was in front on the post. Certainly neither deserved to lose.

Skymas had earlier prepared the crowds for a tumultuous afternoon by giving up to 21lb to his eight rivals and one of the bravest performances of his career. After helping to force a strong gallop, Skymas was struggling in fourth place approaching the penultimate fence and apparently beaten when only fifth over the last. But he launched an amazing rally on the run-in to score, in the end, going away by half a length. The magnitude of that victory is underlined by the fact that no horse since has won the traditional National Day opener carrying within half a stone as much as Skymas. It prepared racegoers for a day that they would never forget – the day that Red Rum competed in his fifth successive Grand National and, in boosting his mindboggling record to three wins and two seconds, displayed a degree of dominance unmatched by any other horse in the history of the race. Already a household name, Red Rum was indeed a legend in his own lifetime. Most steeplechasers are on the decline at the age of twelve but here he was as bright and enthusiastic as ever. He looked a picture of health in the paddock before the National and, before capturing the coveted race yet again, deservedly picked up the 'best turned out horse' award.

The field for the 1977 Grand National, in which Red Rum carried top weight for the fourth successive year, had the rare and exciting ingredient of a current Cheltenham Gold Cup winner. But, unlike Garrison Savannah, who in 1991 looked certain to complete the first National–Gold Cup double since Golden Miller in 1934, Cheltenham hero Davy Lad got no further than the third fence, where he unshipped his jockey. Thirteen of the forty-two runners had come to grief by Becher's first time round and it was this daunting obstacle on the second circuit that probably determined the destiny of the race. It was here that the favourite Andy Pandy, leading the field by a dozen lengths and showing not the slightest sign of fatigue, overbalanced on landing and tantalizingly tottered for a couple of strides before finally losing his legs. Tommy Stack had seemed unflustered as Andy Pandy and John Burke blazed the trail but, with them gone, stepped Rummy up a gear. Though the gallant Churchtown Boy, winner of the Topham Trophy over a circuit of the National course just forty-eight hours earlier, looked mighty dangerous, his chance evaporated when he hit the second last. He could find no more as Red Rum surged clear for a magnificent victory by twenty-five lengths.

It was one of the greatest spectacles in steeplechasing history; but, tragically, two horses paid with their lives. Zeta's Son, with his broken leg, was not the only casualty: Winter Rain, a talented nine-year-old trained by Tony Dickinson and ridden by his son Michael, broke his neck at Becher's first time round.

So I was reeling with mixed emotions as I wearily steered the car back down the M6 motorway that evening. I was grieving for two of jumping's leading lights; but I knew that, along with the thousands at Aintree and millions in front of their television sets, I had just witnessed a day at the races the like of which we shall never experience again.

John de Moraville, whose late father was a racehorse trainer, has been a member of the Daily Express *racing team since 1974, writing mostly under the* nom de plume *of 'Bendex'. He also works as a commentator's assistant for BBC Television.*

Jonathan Powell
QUESTIONS AND ANSWERS

Visiting Aintree for the first time to cover the Grand National for the *News of the World* exceeded my wildest dreams. The race had consumed me since I had won a year's supply of sweets on ESB as a little boy. Already I was bewitched by the possibilities of betting. The next year I tried an extraordinarily ambitious treble involving Sundew in the Grand National, Cambridge in the Boat Race and my hero Dai Dower against Pascual Perez for the world flyweight title. The first two won but poor Dai was knocked out in the first round in Buenos Aires. Much later Fred Winter and Kilmore put a decisive end to my career as the school bookie.

Walking the National course that first time in 1970 I was overawed both by the massive fences and by the endlessly cheerful banter of the doughty riders who prepared to attack them on the morrow. Never mind the view of the hardy old professionals that the fences and the race had gone soft. They looked positively lethal to me. Stakes as thick as a wrestler's biceps standing rigidly like tall sentries covered in bountiful supplies of spruce and gorse. I could not believe that anyone could possibly wish to jump that first gaping ditch in cold blood.

Soon some of those fearless jockeys became friends rather than mere business contacts. The following year I shared with Bob Champion a room no larger than a broom cupboard in a hotel at Southport that made Fawlty Towers seem a model of efficiency. The food was awful and the service non-existent but since many jockeys and trainers stayed there the evening's diversions offered rich compensation. During that first visit to Southport I vividly recall Frenchie (or was it David?) Nicholson nimbly scaling a tall pillar in the lounge on the wrong side of midnight. Several jockeys displayed inordinate strength by walking the length of the dining room with exaggerated handstands clutching, would you believe, champagne bottles in both fists. Naturally they had emptied them first.

Bob's first ride in the Grand National, in 1971, ended abruptly at the very first fence where he was brought down on Country Wedding. He picked himself up, relieved to be in one piece, and limped across to the finishing post in time to see Specify snatch an improbable victory from young Jim Dreaper on Black Secret.

Despite the shambles in Southport Bob and I returned to the same hotel year after year. Now in those days the needs of racing journalists came bottom of the list of a racecourse's priorities. (They still do at some courses, but that is another story.) What was laughingly known as the Liverpool press room boasted a total of four tables, seven chairs – some with seats still attached – and three telephones to accommodate the massed ranks of writers who assembled to cover the world's most famous steeplechase. Usually the second-best race of the afternoon was our own competitive dash to the petrol station on the nearby main road that boasted a precious public callbox. More experienced journalists, like John Oaksey, had an arrangement with local householders. Newcomers like myself had to sprint to the garage, though on one memorable occasion I was asked to leave the forecourt halfway through dictating my copy.

In 1971 Bob Champion waited patiently while I filed my report; then we set off for home. After dinner and a few drinks, Bob was assuring everyone who would listen, 'I would definitely have won.' By the end of the evening he began to believe it himself. Our annual stay in Southport and his determined assault on the Grand National both developed into a triumph of optimism over experience. The facilities at the hotel improved to critical. Each year as we drove south on Saturday night we would say never again. Once, indeed, we defected to the Holiday Inn in the heart of Liverpool. The next time we returned joyously to Southport.

After another disaster on Country Wedding in 1972, Bob's appetite for the Grand National was fired by a remarkable ride the following year on the 100–1 shot Hurricane Rock, in the race which will be for ever remembered for the thunderous late charge that took Red Rum ahead of Crisp in the shadow of the post. Three fences from home Bob Champion was rather surprised to find himself moving into third place on Hurricane Rock. They were still

third jumping the last fence but faded into sixth place at the finish.
That was one year when even Bob did not claim he should have
won. He was sixth again in 1975, on Manicou Bay, fourteenth on
Money Market the next year, and fell at the first fence on Spittin
Image in 1977. More falls followed: on Shifting Gold for young
Kim Bailey in 1978 and on Purdo, at the first fence, in 1979. Like so
many jockeys before and since, Bob was buoyed up in his
extravagant dreams by the belief that his luck at Liverpool would
change next year.

Then came the dreadful news that he was suffering from cancer.
Without treatment, he was told, he would be dead within eight
months. Josh Gifford, bless him, assured Bob his job would remain
open however long he took to recover. Many compassionate men
might have said the same. Few, I suspect, would have fulfilled the
promise in similarly testing circumstances.

Those of us who travelled regularly to Bob's bedside at the Royal
Marsden Hospital at Sutton in Surrey did not, in all conscience,
believe he would ride again; but even at his lowest ebb Bob clung
stubbornly to his conviction that he would return as a jockey. He
had this absurd desire, you see, to ride a horse called Aldaniti in the
Grand National. We would happily have settled for his recovery,
however long it took, even if it cost him his career. His indomitable
spirit dictated otherwise.

At times, wracked by pain from the harsh drugs that ultimately
saved his life, he looked dreadfully ill. Sometimes when I drove him
gently back to Wiltshire for a break with his sister he would ask me
to stop quickly so that he could be sick by the roadside. During
those grim days Bob vomited constantly, suffered horribly from
constipation for days on end, lost all his hair and almost three stone
in weight. He alone believed he would ride again. Stubborn,
certainly; intransigent and downright difficult at times: he would
lose his temper if we even hinted at the possibility of life outside
racing. Sometimes between treatments he would venture out to a
race meeting sporting a fetching wig. Though far from well, he
particularly wanted to see Aldaniti's first run of the season at
Sandown in November 1979. Imagine his feelings when the horse
was pulled up badly lame. Aldaniti's injured leg was put in plaster
for three weeks and his old jockey left the course numb with despair
at this latest hideous misfortune. The loyal Monty Court, then of

the *Sunday Mirror,* lived nearby at Purley and visited Bob almost every day in hospital. After that setback Bob was even less communicative than usual. Monty asked quietly if there was anything he could do to help. A long pause ensued before the stricken jockey whispered: 'Please go away and leave me alone.'

On 1 January 1980 Bob Champion left hospital for the last time, so weak he could hardly walk. The treatment had ended, but during that long, cold winter the nightmare continued. Worst of all, when he tried to ride his niece's pony he discovered that he could not hold the reins properly since he had lost most of the feeling in his hands and feet. His recovery was agonizingly slow, but at least he put back all the lost weight. At the end of March he insisted on travelling to Aintree for the 1980 Grand National. We stayed in Southport again and he assured everyone he would be back on Aldaniti in 1981. Few, I know, believed him.

Soon he was on his way to a warmer climate in America to continue his battle for fitness. There, on 31 May 1980, he won on his comeback ride on the flat at Fairhill, Maryland. I reported the story with bursting pride and unashamed bias that weekend in the *Sunday People.*

It was after that heartwarming triumph that publishers began to take an interest in Bob's comeback. We discussed several options and agreed to sign a joint contract with Victor Gollancz. I would deliver the manuscript at the end of March 1981; the final chapter would be the Grand National. At that stage it seemed an implausible conclusion. By late July he was ready to continue his rehabilitation at home.

Josh Gifford recalls: 'Bob would call me and say, "You don't want me yet, do you? I'm just going off to Virginia." And I would say "Have a nice time and give her my love"!'

When Bob did return to England he won on Physicist at Fontwell for Josh Gifford late in September. Other races raised serious doubts about his ability to ride as effectively as before. Lack of feeling in his hands continually hampered his method of slipping his reins landing over fences. His weight, too, was a constant problem. The sauna at Hungerford became his second home. With Josh Gifford's horses out of form some owners insisted on employing the younger Richard Rowe. By December Bob Champion's much-heralded comeback had reached crisis point. Rides were increasingly scarce, winners bleakly elusive. Wherever I turned I was aware of people muttering that Bob had 'gone'. Josh Gifford was under intense pressure to replace him, but remained resolutely loyal despite his own private misgivings. What Bob needed most was plenty of practice and a change of luck.

It came at Ascot on 13 December. Within the space of forty minutes he was triumphant on Kybo and Henry Bishop in the day's two main steeplechases. Both were trained by Josh Gifford. The drought was over. In February Bob Champion rode Aldaniti once more, at Ascot. Back in training after a lengthy absence, the chestnut with the almost tangible will to win offered his old jockey renewed hope in the Grand National by storming to victory in the Whitbread Trial Chase. In the circumstances it was a wonderfully encouraging return and a triumph touched with elegance. What, Bob reasoned, could possibly beat them at Liverpool if the horse remained sound? His enthusiasm was so infectious that I rushed to accept the odds of 33–1 offered by Corals against Aldaniti winning at Aintree. Displaying a rare degree of impartiality I advised Julian Wilson and Brough Scott to do likewise.

Once again we took the road to Southport, more hopeful than ever before. Early on Saturday morning we walked the course with Josh, Althea and Nicky Gifford; Nick and Valda Embiricos, who had been unfailingly loyal in their desire to see Bob ride Aldaniti in this race above all; the four Embiricos children; Henry Pelham; and the Giffords' lively terrier Rocky. My very certain recollection of that eventful inspection of the daunting fences was that Josh wanted his jockey to hunt round for at least a circuit before beginning his move towards the leaders.

By now the manuscript of *Champion's Story* had been safely delivered to Gollancz. This would be the last chapter. Jack Knight, a fine photographer and good friend, was signed up for the day with the explicit instructions: 'Go down to the final fence and take a photograph of Aldaniti jumping it even if he is in last place'! So much for this author's confidence.

Unless you are watching the Grand National on television, following the race, even with binoculars, is a challenging exercise. The runners gallop further away from the stands at Aintree than any other course in the world. Accordingly, those of us who report on this great race annually spend most of the time with our backs to the course as we perch high on the windswept roof that is our time-honoured position. The reason for this apparent indifference is that we are watching an invaluable television monitor hanging precariously from a beam at the rear of the stand. Once the runners are on their way we turn round only to witness them jump the Chair and water and then again for the final lung-sapping run to the line at the end of the second circuit.

So it was with some alarm that I spotted on our lone monitor Aldaniti surging irresistibly into the lead as early as the twelfth fence, far sooner than his jockey intended or his trainer planned. There was bleak consolation in the manner of his bold, accurate jumping. Though I say it myself, normally I am a perfectly sound race-reader: not on this occasion, with emotion already engulfing me. The longer Aldaniti stayed ahead the more certain I was that he would be caught before the end of that long, pitiless run-in. Royal Mail, ridden by another close friend Philip Blacker, offered a constant threat for much of the final mile. More ominously, once Aldaniti had crossed the last fence safely, I could see through my tears the doughty Spartan Missile and his veteran rider John Thorne finishing with a rare intensity of purpose.

The final furlong of that unforgettable race seemed to last for ever. During the time it takes for weary steeplechasers to cover two hundred and twenty yards I was assailed by a maelstrom of emotions. Beside me I was vaguely aware that Monty Court, too, was all but overcome as the drama reached a crescendo of excitement. Shaking uncontrollably, unwilling to witness the hideous certainty of Spartan Missile overtaking Aldaniti, in those final heart-stopping moments I cowered behind the bulky presence of my good friend Tony Stafford of the *Daily Telegraph*. He it was, fine judge, who kept insisting through the bedlam that Aldaniti was holding on. I dared not look again until he lifted my head in time for me to see Bob Champion raise his arm in his moment of victory.

I stumbled down the steep steps, tears coursing over my face, and rushed headlong towards the winner's enclosure as if in a trance. Jack Knight would have the photograph of a lifetime. The last chapter, too, no longer seemed such a problem; indeed, it eventually overflowed into three chapters. Everyone lucky enough to be present that day knew that they had been touched by one of those precious moments which transcend the narrow theatre of sport. Has there ever been a finer essay in resilience?

Though my mind was in turmoil I gathered my thoughts sufficiently in the post-race chaos of the crowded press room to write the happiest story I have ever filed. That evening Bob, his fiancée Jo and I drove back down the M6, all three of us squeezed into the front seats of his car, anxious not to break the spell. Later that night we were guests at a dinner thrown by John Thorne. The epitome of a sporting English gentleman, he generously put aside his own disappointment at finishing so close on Spartan Missile and applauded the towering performance of his valiant friend Bob Champion on Aldaniti.

We did not reach home until long after midnight. The next morning my wife Charlotte told me gently that Bill Lovelace, my close schoolfriend who had done so much to foster my interest in racing, had died from a brain tumour the previous Thursday. Thoughtfully she had kept the grim news from me at Liverpool. Three days after the Grand National we buried Bill on a golden spring day at the ancient church next to his home in a timeless Dorset village. Afterwards his wife Jane and two little girls looked unbearably young as they walked bravely through the churchyard. It was a time for asking questions that you knew could never be answered.

Jonathan Powell has been a racing journalist for over 20 years and is now the racing correspondent of the Sunday Express. *He is the author of two bestsellers –* Champion's Story *and* Desert Orchid *– and was named Racing Journalist of the Year in 1981.*

Paul Hayward
HISTORY RATTLES THE BONES

Racing had probably never been so important. Such was the feeling as 38,000 Germans converged on Hoppegarten racecourse for the first East–West meeting since the Berlin Wall was raised in 1961. It's not often that our sport acts as a filter, a lens, for great political shifts in world affairs.

Unification was in motion that last weekend in March 1990 and the people of Berlin and beyond knew that the union of two worlds for an apparently simple purpose would provide knowledge about a daunting but nevertheless inviting future. Somebody said the two countries were circling each other like an awkward, nerve-ridden courting couple, and it was easy to recognize the disparities on the drive down Karl-Marx-Allee in East Berlin. For days, metallic blue Mercedes glided past the filth-belching Skodas and Trabants; inside were sponsors, money men and speculators making the ten-mile journey to one of the finest recreational venues of the Weimar period.

A forlorn place. Or so it was that Friday as Artur Böhlke, head of racing in the East, worked to restore the course to its pre-Cold War augustness. It was a day of pale sunlight, which cast a gentle radiance on the flaking paintwork and cracking stucco of the grandstand, where Goering and other psychopaths of the Third Reich would sit for lunch as the top thoroughbreds of the Nazi era performed their unwitting rounds. When it was said that the leading figures in Hitler's regime came here at weekends, we greeted the information with scepticism. But then we saw the photographs, offered by a shrunken woman clutching a sun-curled album. They told us the course had ossified under communism and that Goering would recognize the place even now. Thankfully, there was no pleasure in these voices.

For twenty-nine years only the scraggy, state-owned horses of the East had galloped round this broad track. Böhlke was the archetypal dissident in hiding, hating the constraints the racing industry operated under and waiting, like many East Germans, for the pall of totalitarianism to lift. He had turned grey waiting, though the greased quiff and leather jacket were indications that a connection with *elsewhere* had been preserved. In front of the main stand, two workers were unloading wooden chairs from a tumbril, anchored by a sullen Shire horse. You began to fear for the organizers of this experiment, should those 38,000 Germans honk and nudge down the narrow roads for a day at the races. Back to the city we went, David Ashdown, the photographer, and I, hoping not to make the navigational error of the outward trip, when we narrowly avoided driving down the throat of a Soviet military base.

In the papers were stories of mass graves being uncovered in the forests. There were accounts, too, of atrocities by the Stasi, the secret police, who were said to have an informer in every household. Böhlke had told us there were a handful at Hoppegarten. He had known who they were, and avoided any transgression that would have threatened his life. Berlin was a city waking to memory, and few of the recollections engendered cheer. We bought Russian hats and badges, feeling as if we were crawling through James Dean's car to yank a memento off the dashboard. Metronomically, people beat at the Wall with hammers and chisels, breaking off fragments of an insanity. Television has digested and finished with these images now, but to be in Berlin that weekend – for the races, for God's sake – was to feel history rattling the bones.

Never travel with clichéd expectations. At the track in the morning the traffic was efficiently and courteously directed into car parks. A quiet revolution, of the Western kind, had descended overnight. Hoardings and marquees had appeared on the lawns, exhortations to consume had been placed where they always are: where television's eye can see them. Mercedes' flags flapped in the breeze; a Coca-Cola hot air balloon was being inflated by roars of gas. In East Berlin there was still no advertising to be seen; here it was everywhere (there was even an advisory clinic for the Berliner Bank). So obvious was it that capitalism's predatory instincts had been aroused by this meeting, the gathering was an almost banal illustration of the days ahead for post-communist Germany. It

198

offered the West as a dream to people who were trying to escape the myths of systems and ideologies.

There was concern about the East German horses. For the most part they were competing on equal terms with runners from the more prosperous stables of West Germany and it was feared the contrast in quality would be as stark as it had been on the roads. Whoever designed the Trabant car, whichever politicians decided it was acceptable for the air to be fouled that way, should be hauled before the international courts.

The *Independent*'s enterprise in dispatching us to Berlin was about to be rewarded. The only other British journalists at Hoppegarten were Brough Scott, who had produced an earlier piece for the *Sunday Times* but was there a second time purely for his own enjoyment, and David Connolly-Smith, representing the *Racing Post*. We were advised to keep a look-out for Lutz Mader, the jockey who was caught trying to swim a river to escape the East, imprisoned for nine months and finally sold to the West for hard currency. It was 1974 when they fished him from the water, and this was his homecoming.

'It's exactly the way I left it all those years ago,' he said in the Weimaresque weighing room. He looked uncomfortable, perhaps fearing that the old ways would reassert themselves before the afternoon was out and he would be dragged off to gaol once more. But his return produced a pleasing symmetry. Steam rose from the crowds as they pressed against the rails, but through the bodies and children-on-shoulders you could see Mader's silks popping from a moving swarm of riders and horses. It was the first race and Mader was winning it. The end of a sixteen-year exile. A race as a means of at once remembering and forgetting. 'I've been waiting a long time for this,' he said later. 'We all have. Time has stood still here. But it will get better.' He was still strangely pallid.

But was it like a wedding? Not to the Easterners who booed when Mader made that surge. There were only a few, but enough to remind us that not everyone here saw the transition to a Western society as a route to salvation. Hans-Heinrich von Loeper, a visiting West German official, had said: 'The most important purpose is that people from both sides come together after forty years. The happenings on the Turf are not so important.' Yet this ultra-smart man was dispassionate and straight-faced enough in his delivery for you to believe that absorption, not integration, was on the cards. Hoppegarten was Germany's Newmarket or Chantilly, a place where kaisers had come before the Nazis. And there were Germans in the West who wanted it back.

Mader's triumph loaded the day with the happy symbolism of the times, but for the briefest period. That race was confined to horses trained in the East, and the time was approaching when the two sides would meet, perhaps with cruel consequences. In the first of these contests the first five finishers came from stables in the West. Half an hour later, the first four. Then the first six. It made you think of a boxing match in which the referee had failed, or refused, to rescue a battered and weakening protagonist. The mood grew more sullen as melancholy set in among the Easterners and embarrassment amid those from the West. There was no triumphalism, and as the races flicked over it was the taking of food and drink, the exploratory looks, that took precedence. Racing had performed its task in bringing two halves of a city together, but nobody wanted it to go on reiterating lessons that had already been absorbed.

A racecourse is a gambling den, yet here people stood off the bookmakers, perhaps because austerity's grip was still strong; possibly, and more prosaically, form on the page meant little when horses were meeting for the first time.

This was before the single currency and political union. It preceded full freedom of movement. It drew a city on to a racecourse to help dissolve the mutual alienation the Wall had manufactured. We stood in a West German beer tent and drank to an uncertain future, wary, perhaps, of the displays of nationalism in a place where Nazism had holidayed, but with a sense of gratitude at being here at all. It was one of those days the mind recalls at nights.

Paul Hayward is racing correspondent of the Independent. *He joined the paper from the* Racing Post *in December 1989, and is a contributor to television and radio. He lives in Brighton.*

Sean Magee
AT BELMONT WITH THE HORSE PLAYERS

Light and shade.

Manhattan was bathed in chilly autumnal brightness as we made our way to Penn Station, and the sunshine reflected the mood. This was the Big Day: Belmont Park for the 1990 Breeders' Cup, the world championships of racing. Down to the subterranean gloom of the platform to crowd into the carriages, and out into the light again after a few hundred yards.

As soon as the train pulled out, the horse players swung into action, spreading out their copies of the *Daily Racing Form* and unsheathing their felt-tips and their ball-points and their highlight pens. Red, blue and black ink encircled the key elements of the form. The enlightened highlighted their fancies with orange, yellow, green and pink. The still benighted chewed their pencils and studied hard.

Those of us there just for the sport had less pressing need to ponder the form, so we spent the journey chattering about the heroic deeds we were about to witness. Dayjur, the fastest horse in Europe for many a year, faced his greatest challenge in the Sprint. Arc hero Saumarez and Coronation Cup winner In The Wings were to clash in the Turf. The Classic had the Kentucky Derby winner Unbridled pitched against another top American three-year-old Rhythm, Ireland's Belmont Stakes hero Go And Go, the Canadian Isvestia, and dear old Ibn Bey from England – surely out of his depth in such company. There would be a dream Mile with Royal Academy, Steinlen, Priolo, Markofdistinction and Distant Relative. The filly Meadow Star and the colt Fly So Free were American two-year-olds which we'd heard were something special. And the race about which the local horse players were really tingling was the Distaff showdown between Bayakoa and Go For Wand, the filly

201

whose elegant form was printed large on the front of the second section of the *Racing Form* and who most of our neighbours in that carriage felt would provide the equine star turn of the day. This would be some race meeting.

At the track we poured out, all bright-eyed with anticipation. No, not quite all. As I made my way to the Clubhouse entrance I encountered one disgruntled horse player making straight back to the train. 'Five dollars? I ain't payin' five dollars! It's always four dollars!' For Breeders' Cup day grandstand entrance did indeed cost one dollar more than for an ordinary Belmont day – around £2.50 to get in rather than £2 – and this player wasn't playing along with that. Let him go his sulky way: this was no day for mean spirits.

Nor was it a day for the inappropriately dressed. New York society may be a melting pot, but the racecard proclaimed the demand for decorum. No 'abbreviated attire' in the Clubhouse, please, and on the Garden Terrace 'absolutely no jeans, designer or otherwise'. Even in the Grandstand, 'Shirts and shoes required'. You may leave without your shirt, but you'd better be wearing it going in.

My own shirt was to be plonked on Distant Relative in the Mile, but I was informed by a charmingly sympathetic lady at a betting window that Barry Hills' colt had been scratched, and I'd better find some other way of financing my visit. Mulling this over, I met up with my friend the Professor of Political Science at the University of Massachusetts – the horse players come from all walks of life – and advised him that Relief Pitcher would win the second race of the day, the latter of two events preliminary to the Breeders' Cup itself. After Pat Eddery's mount had obliged, the sun shone yet more brightly.

The first Cup race was the Sprint, six furlongs on dirt. My idea was to have a good look at Dayjur in the paddock, but the rhythms of racegoing in the USA are different from in Europe, and paddock inspection for ordinary horse players mainly involved watching the massed ranks of the elite inside the ring – graced by a statue of the incomparable Secretariat at full stretch. The attention of those on the inside was focused on the saddling boxes, where the runners in each race were assembled and mounted before taking two quick turns of the paddock itself and then walking out onto the track. The rest of us watched the privileged watching the horses, but even the briefest glimpse of Dayjur proclaimed that he was ready to defy the circumstances packed against him.

Those circumstances were run through by course commentator Tom Durkin as the runners for the Sprint were being loaded into the starting gate: 'Dayjur has never run on dirt – indeed he has never raced around a turn.' This amused the horse players greatly, and they tittered and chuckled: what on earth was this Limey animal doing here against the best sprinters in America? Away on the far side of the track, the object of their derision seemed to resent being cast as a clown. Awash with sweat, he was reluctant to be loaded into the stalls, and – worst of all – he missed the break.

As the runners scorched round the far bend something odd happened. One horse clawed the air and fell, another slammed into it. But leave that, look at Dayjur. Pumped along by Willie Carson to make up the vital lengths lost at the start, he forced the laughter of the horse players back through their teeth as he came flying round the bend to join issue with the filly Safely Kept. She had been narrowly beaten in the Sprint in 1989, but Dayjur wore her down as the pair hammered up the stretch. Safely Kept had the rail but Dayjur the upper hand. Clearly he was going to win. Hard by Manhattan, we grabbed a Gershwin line: Ho ho ho, who's got the last laugh now?

The Fates had. Bright sunshine throws dark shadows, and the timekeeper's box on top of the stand a hundred yards from the wire had printed a solid black rectangle on the dirt. Suddenly this was in Dayjur's path, and he did what came naturally: he jumped it. His finishing thrust was destroyed, and though he tried to rally, he propped at another shadow right on the line and Safely Kept won by a neck.

Robbed! Easing Dayjur down, Willie Carson shook his head in exasperated recognition of one of the craziest hard-luck stories ever, and taking the cue, the bewildered horse players shook their heads in unison. They had never seen anything like it, never seen a major horse race so prey to a caprice of the weather: twenty minutes either side of post time, and that shadow would have been well out of Dayjur's way. The visitors knew that the colt had been startled by some imagined threat at the end of his last race, the Prix de l'Abbaye, but to be deprived in such fashion of what would have been the greatest victory of an English-trained horse on foreign soil was just too much. Scratching our heads and muttering like the demented souls we had left behind on the streets of the city, we wandered inside to find solace in beer and hot dogs. Nobody said, 'That's racing.'

But the show must go on. The Juvenile Fillies held no bizarre surprises, Meadow Star cruising home just as expected. Then came the contest that for all Americans was the main event. Even allowing for the late withdrawal of Gorgeous, the Breeders' Cup Distaff promised to be the race of the day – or of the year, of the decade. It presented a duel between Go For Wand, queen of the three-year-old fillies and winner of her last five races, and the six-year-old Bayakoa, who had won the Distaff at Gulfstream Park a year before.

This was a head-to-head clash to drool over, even for us visitors who were less familiar than the natives with the nuances of the form, and the race was barely a few yards old before we knew that expectations would not be disappointed. Shooting out of the starting gate on the back stretch, Go For Wand held an early lead, but was rapidly joined by Bayakoa on her outside. Neck and neck, the two took each other on down the far side, and came round the bend into the home stretch with nothing between them. It was a classic contest, one surely destined to join the famous encounters between Affirmed and Alydar, Ferdinand and Alysheba, Easy Goer and Sunday Silence in the list of mammoth American races.

Those unforgettable duels had claimed their place in a book about great races I had recently written, and as this latest pair of eyeball-to-eyeball battlers came thundering round the bend and straightened up for home, I started to compose the lines which would be needed in some future edition. For by anyone's standards, this was one of the greatest.

Go For Wand on the rails, Bayakoa on her outside, the two came barrelling down the stretch towards us, locked together, neither flinching. Around me the horse players were going berserk with excitement, whether they had backed Go For Wand or Bayakoa or (like me) neither. For a second Bayakoa seemed to have her junior's measure, then Go For Wand came back at her. This time the lines were from another song: something's gotta give, something's gotta give, something's gotta give . . .

The climax of any horse race is not the winning post but the instant before the resolution becomes apparent, and the truly great races elongate that moment to the point where you want the action to freeze and leave you with the raw essence of the contest itself. So it was now, but what broke the deadlock was something infinitely more awful than one horse capitulating. With less than a hundred yards to run and the outcome still suspended in that magic moment, Go For Wand stretched a foreleg an inch further than nature had designed, crashed to the ground and turned a horrific somersault into the rails. As Bayakoa galloped on to win a hollow prize, Go For Wand struggled up, but the worst was hideously obvious. Her off foreleg had snapped just above the fetlock, which she swung uselessly and accusingly at us. In the few seconds that it took the filly to hobble towards the stand, the glory of Breeders' Cup Day 1990 blew out into the Long Island air like a burst balloon.

To describe the effect of Go For Wand's fall, you grope for analogies. A shadow had passed over the sun. The party's over. But no metaphor will properly encapsulate that moment. Its most immediate manifestation was the sound. The hollering of fifty thousand people yelling the horses home modulated in an instant to a massive collective gasp which swelled into a scream then diminished into a gabbled wailing, as the horse players gawped at the most awful sight they would ever see on a racetrack.

The practicalities were dealt with expeditiously. An outrider immobilized the stricken filly, screens were erected, she was dispatched, and a massive white horse ambulance was parked in front of the Clubhouse for her removal.

How could the horse players cope with this? They watched with ghoulish compulsion as the ambulance hurried the body of Go For Wand away. And then they clung there in the stands, struck dumb by the intrusion of true catastrophe at their celebration. Some were wiping their eyes, or pinching the top of their noses to stem the tears. Never mind the image of American racing fans as hardened gamblers, mere players of the numbers. This was something else. Plenty were crying outright. Others just stared blankly towards the infield.

In moments of true crisis, attempts to press on with the demands of normality take on a bizarre unreality. The Distaff had been sponsored by Consort Hair Spray – 'A Sure Bet for Great-Looking

Hair' – and within minutes of the disaster a meek, balding little man in glasses, the General Manager of Consort's parent company Alberto-Culver USA Incorporated, had the hapless task of presenting the trophy to the connections of Bayakoa, no less shattered and tearful than anyone else around the winner's circle, a few feet from where Go For Wand had just breathed her last. The General Manager had rehearsed his lines carefully, and delivered them with dogged determination: 'On behalf of the Alberto-Culver company, and its sponsoring brand for today's race, Consort Hair-Care Products for Men, we are pleased to present you the trophy for this year's Breeders' Cup Distaff. Congratulations.'

Back inside the stand, the television presenters were lost for words: 'What can we say?', a commentator was asking. Nothing. There was nothing to say.

I stumbled into the gents. The death of Go For Wand had followed that of Mr Nickerson in the Sprint: that was what had happened on the bend in Dayjur's race (and Shaker Knit, the horse who had cannoned into the stricken Mr Nickerson, was put down later that evening). The rest room seethed with unrest: 'This isn't a racetrack,' someone yelled, 'it's a junk yard!'

My friend the Professor, as befits his calling, was more analytical. He had watched the Distaff inside the stand, seated with serried ranks of horse players on benches and viewing the race on a large television screen. Why not go the extra few yards and see it live? 'The race on television was a simulacrum of how TV homogenises experience.' (Whoo! They don't talk like that at Plumpton!)

But forget analysis: now was the time for emotion. The death of a horse in any race causes revulsion and guilt: is the enjoyment we harvest from racing worth such moments? We'd searched our souls for the correct response at Cheltenham and at Liverpool, but this was different. Here calamity had gate-crashed at the very peak of the action, and it was a uniquely sickening experience. If *that*'s racing, you can keep it.

Battered by repeated viewings of the horror on the screens inside the stand, we wandered down to the paddock for the next race, the Mile. Here was a sight to provide distraction if anything could: Lester Piggott back in the saddle after retiring in 1985. His comeback ride in England had taken place only the previous week, and here he was on Royal Academy, trained by his old comrade-in-arms Vincent O'Brien. The most noticeable difference from the Lester of old was that he grinned a lot, as if sharing our disbelief that this comeback was really happening. But a vociferous contingent of the horse players believed it well enough, cheering the 54-year-old grandfather round the paddock and going quite delirious with excitement after he had brought Royal Academy sweeping up the stands side for a last-gasp victory. Here was Piggott at the height of his powers just a few days after his return to action, and, if only for a few moments, he brought back the sunshine.

A minor handicap would have been just the job to steady the stomach after the emotional roller-coaster that Breeders' Cup Day 1990 had become. Instead it was time for the Juvenile, won by the favourite Fly So Free, and then the Turf, a race which under calmer circumstances would have had us bubbling with expectation – Saumarez, In The Wings, Cacoethes, With Approval. Now it was just another rich dish plonked before us when indigestion and queasiness were setting in and what we really wanted was to wave away the waiter, or, if we must, nibble on a dry biscuit. In The Wings won with authority, but the glory of the day was fading with the light.

The horse players beetled back inside to place their bets on the last race, and as if in inarticulate protest that this day had been too much, a drunk in the back row of the Clubhouse slammed both feet against the empty seat in front of him, spraying his indignant neighbours with a shrapnel of plastic.

By the time of the $3,000,000 Classic – the world's richest race – most of the horse players were drained. Though the Classic was a marvellous race, with Unbridled surging back to form and Paul Cole's Ibn Bey turning in a gargantuan performance to run him to a length, it was too late in the day. We'd had Dayjur and Meadow Star and Lester, but most of all we'd had Go For Wand. Enough was enough.

As I left the track and wandered away trying to make sense of it all, I passed one of the horse players engaged in a furious altercation with a seller of tee-shirts: the shirt he had just bought was too small, the guy had to change it. The tee-shirt seller's response was to run off, but the other man chased after him and continued to remonstrate. The seller ran off again, still pursued by his aggrieved customer, and the pair disappeared into the twilight.

Soon Breeders' Cup Day 1990 slid into just another New York Sunday morning, and we talked over the events of the day as we sank nightcap after nightcap, squeezing the very last drop from the most extraordinary day's racing there had ever been. Was it the best of days, or the worst of days? The brightest or the darkest? Like that seller of tee-shirts sprinting into the gloom away from the disgruntled horse player, the answer was elusive.

So the early hours found me sipping just one final whisky and leafing through the day's racecard, reliving the dizzying ups and downs. Dayjur, Lester Piggott, Meadow Star, Unbridled – they had all etched lasting memories. But each time I closed my eyes the image that burned ineradicably was that of the vast white horse ambulance, driving slowly off the track with the carcass of Go For Wand.

All over New York, the horse players were having the same nightmare.

Sean Magee wrote The Channel Four Book of Racing *in 1989 while spending the daylight hours as an academic publisher, and the following year* The Channel Four Book of the Racing Year *and* Great Races *accelerated his shift from publishing to full-time writing. He is also editor of* The Channel Four Racing Companion *and has compiled* Oaksey on Racing *and* The Daily Telegraph Flat Racing Yearbook.